DISNEY UNIVERSE

PRIMA Official Game Guide

CONTENTS

WELCOME TO THE DISNEY UNIVERSE

Disney Universe was created to allow people to enter virtual worlds of their favorite Disney movies. VIC, a Virtual Information Cube, is your tour guide. You get to suit up and play in legendary Disney and Disney.Pixar worlds. The *Disney Universe* is a completely safe and dependable system, allowing you to experience thrills and chills with absolutely no danger whatsoever. The cast bots transport you on a journey into the Disney worlds of your dreams. The bots are completely safe. They couldn't hurt you if they wanted to. . . .

Taking over!

However, just as the *Disney Universe* lets in its first guests, it is taken over by HEX—the boss of bosses. He now owns the system and runs things. He is ready to rock, roll, and reboot. The bots are now under his control. You must travel through several different worlds and defeat HEX's bots and bosses to rescue the guests they have captured.

THE WORLDS OF THE DISNEY UNIVERSE

Each world in the *Disney Universe* consists of three locations.

Pirates of the Caribbean

You start out your adventures in the *Disney Universe* in the city of London. Make your way to the docks and sink a pirate ship to free the first guest.

After completing the London location in the *Pirates of the Caribbean* world, you must then rescue a guest who has been taken on Blackbeard's pirate ship, the *Queen Anne's Revenge*.

The final location here is the Fountain of Youth. You must get to the fountain and collect mermaid tears to free another guest.

Don't forget to play through each location a second time to rescue another guest and unlock a new costume.

Alice

After stumbling into the world of Wonderland, you must follow the White Rabbit through the garden to rescue a guest.

Next, make your way through the castle of the Red Queen, fighting enemies and freeing another guest.

Having completed the Red Castle location, you must now make your way across the castle grounds to find the trapped guest.

Lion King

You are now in the African savannah as you fight your way around Lower Pride Rock to find a guest to save.

Lost in the Elephant Graveyard, you must find a way to reach the guest trapped in a cage and free him.

Now that you are at Pride Rock, defeat Scar in a final confrontation.

Monsters, Inc.

If you want to rescue the guest on the scream floor at the factory, you must collect canisters of scream and move through teleporting doors.

After being trapped in the Himalayas, get to the village to rescue a trapped guest and then return to the Monstropolis.

Back in the Monster world, get through the offices and then the Door Factory to find the captured guest.

Aladdin

You begin in the Cave of Wonders, where you must find a path to get to the guest and escape.

Jafar has captured a guest. Make your way through the Streets of Agrabah to rescue the guest and get to the palace.

Fight your way through Agrabah Palace and defeat Jafar in a battle to save another guest.

WALL-E

Earth has been abandoned, but you must find a way through the wasteland of refuse to get to the guest.

Make your way through several levels on board the *Axiom* as you chase after the precious plant in a boot and rescue a guest.

Get the *Axiom* back to Earth by defeating Auto, the ship's wheel, and then save the guest.

HOW TO USE THIS GUIDE

Disney Universe is an exciting, action-packed adventure through the worlds of Disney movies. This guide has been specially designed to provide all of the information you need to rescue the guests in each of the worlds, find all the collectibles, and unlock all the costumes.

The Walkthrough

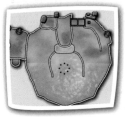

These six chapters provide the direction you need to make it through the six Disney worlds and rescue the guests that HEX has captured. You'll find detailed maps for each level showing locations of all collectibles, items, and power-ups. Not only do you get a detailed walkthrough, both VIC and HEX provide tips to help you get the most out of your experience. As an added bonus, you can also find out which achievements/trophies you can earn as you play through the game so that you don't have to go back and get them later.

Navigating the Universe

While the Disney movies are a lot of fun, they are also filled with danger. You need to know several basic things to survive. This section covers controlling your character and all of the combos and combat moves you need to learn to defeat the enemies. In addition, you get the 411 on all the power-ups you can use, the items and collectibles you can find, and what to do with all the coins you pick up. *Disney Universe* is even more fun when playing with other players. Therefore, this guide gives you tips on how to play together as a team as well as how to beat the other players and win. Finally, this chapter covers the different types of challenges you can play during the game.

Costume Shop

There are 45 different costumes available in *Disney Universe*. While you start off with some, the rest must be unlocked and purchased. This chapter shows you all the costumes you can get as well as how to unlock them.

HEX's Bots

HEX has been capturing guests in the *Disney Universe* and is not about to let them go. To prevent you from rescuing these guests, HEX has taken over the bots in the various worlds and now controls them. They are all programmed to stop you. From Flying Fodder to Brutes and Rotos, this chapter covers all of the enemies in the game. Learn about their unique attacks so you can avoid taking damage. Get the scoop on how to beat them.

Secrets and Awards

We have put together this chapter covering secrets and awards to make sure this guide includes everything you could possibly need. Here, we show you how to get all 162 world collectibles, which are found in every single level. You can also find out about all of the achievements and trophies you can earn as you play the game.

PIRATES OF THE CARIBBEAN WALKTHROUGH

When you first begin *Disney Universe*, the Pirates of the Caribbean world is the only one unlocked. Within this world, you must first play the London level, which features three different areas.

Start off by selecting the London level. Then you must choose which costume your character will wear for this first area. There are several costumes to pick from, and you unlock more by completing levels in the game.

Disney TRIVIA

The Pirates of the Caribbean world is based on the movie *Pirates of the Caribbean: On Stranger Tides*, the fourth movie in the series.

Please take note...

This strategy was written for one-to-two players. When playing with more friends (up to four), you may find that some of the puzzles will have very subtle differences.

For example, if a puzzle requires you to stand on a switch before grabbing an object during one-player game play, during multiplayer game play, that same puzzle may require a friend to stand on the switch, while you or another player grabs the object.

LONDON

Level 1

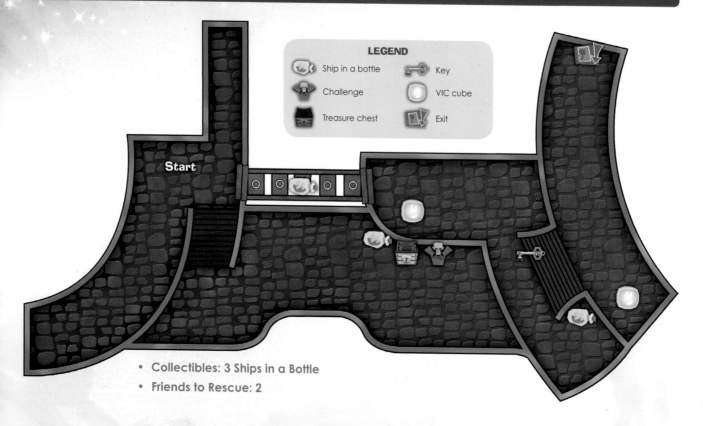

LEGEND

Ship in a bottle — Key

Challenge — VIC cube

Treasure chest — Exit

Start

- Collectibles: 3 Ships in a Bottle
- Friends to Rescue: 2

BUILD THE CANNON

You begin this level on the left side near some crates. Start off by hitting the crates along the left side of the area to release Mickey coins, then head down the stairs to the lower level. Press the Attack button to swing your tool to break the crates.

Mickey coins can be found scattered about the level. You can find more by breaking open objects with your tool and by defeating enemies. Collect these coins to unlock new worlds as well as purchase costumes that are unlocked as you complete the various levels of the game.

There is a limited number of Mickey coins in each area. Therefore, when you are playing with other players, rush to collect the coins before they do. The more you get, the fewer coins are left for the other players.

Once you get down to the lower level, move over to the cannon barrel and hold down the Use button. While holding down this button, you can move the barrel to the right and onto the gun carriage to build the cannon. Now move around this lower area to collect as many coins as possible.

Now shoot at the three targets under the bridge. This causes the platforms of the bridge to swing up and into position so you can cross to the area's right side.

BUILD THE BRIDGE

Climb onto the cannon by pressing the Use button while standing near it. Then drive the cannon around the lower area and shoot at targets. By blowing up the wooden door on the far-right side of this lower area you can get a large coin.

Challenge

Before moving across the bridge, go to the arcade game and press the Use button to start a challenge. Challenges pit you against other players and the clock to earn coins and other awards. An arcade game appears in every level after you accomplish one of the objectives. In this level, it appears after you build the bridge.

SHIP IN A BOTTLE

Shoot the door with the target on it by the bridge to blast it open. Inside you can get the first Ship in a Bottle—one of three collectibles in London.

CROSS THE BRIDGE

Press Ⓐ to jump.

Head up the stairs to the left of the area and then move to the first bridge platform. You must jump across to the second platform. There is a wide gap between the second and third platforms on the bridge. To get across, you must double-jump by tapping the Jump button a second time while in midair. Then continue jumping to get the rest of the way across the bridge.

SHIP IN A BOTTLE

As you perform the double-jump to get across the gap on the bridge, be sure to pick up the second Ship in a Bottle along the way. If you miss it, perform a double jump back to the left and try again.

OPEN THE CASTLE GATE

Collect the blue VIC cubes to receive a Power-Up.

Once you get to the other side of the bridge, you face your first enemies on this level—not counting those from the challenge. Fodder and Flying Fodder come after you. Here is a good chance to practice fighting.

Just after you get across the bridge, pick up the blue VIC cube to receive a Power-Up. These are random, so you never know what you will get. Use the Power-Up to help defeat the enemies.

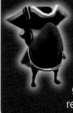

Fodder

Fodder are the basic enemies you face in Disney Universe. They dress up in costumes to fit into their current world. Therefore, in the Pirates of the Caribbean world, they are dressed up like British soldiers. Fodder can be armed with weapons. It takes a few hits to defeat a Fodder, so keep at it. Use more powerful attacks to stun groups of them and then finish them off.

Flying Fodder

Flying fodder are enemies with wings. They can hop around on the ground and also fly up into the air. When they are flying, you must jump up and attack to hit them. This usually stuns them and they drop to the ground, where you can finish them off with regular attacks.

You can make several types of attacks. These are combos created by using the Attack and Jump buttons. Use this fight to try out some of the combos.

Attacks

Attack	Combo (Button Presses)	Description
Simple Attack	Attack	This is the standard attack.
Air Attack	Jump, Attack	Use this to attack when you need to attack an enemy up high.
Ground Slam Attack	Jump, Jump, Attack	Perform a double jump and then press the Attack button. You come down and slam the ground, inflicting damage and stunning nearby enemies.
Uppercut	Hold Attack	Hold down and then release the Attack button once you are airborne. This attack inflicts more damage than a simple attack.
Uppercut and Slam	Hold Attack	Keep holding down the Attack button while airborne and you will perform a ground slam attack.

After defeating the enemies, climb onto the nearby cannon and fire at the targets to start them spinning. After a couple of hits, the castle gates open.

EXIT THE LEVEL

As you move toward the stairs, walk up to the key and press the Use button to pick it up. Now drop down to the lower level to the left and carry the key to the locked treasure chest. More enemies attack, so drop the key and fight back. Then pick up the key again and open the treasure chest using the key to get a star.

Stars are important items and there is a limited number in each level. When you pick up a star, you upgrade the tool for your current costume. You start out with a level 1 tool for each costume. As you increase in levels, your tools cause more damage. Plus, when you do a ground slam attack, upgraded tools have new effects. At level 2, the tools have an electrical effect. Level 3 tools have a fire effect, and level 4 tools have a magical effect.

When playing with other players, let them fight off the enemies while you grab the key and rush for the chest so you can get the star for yourself.

Climb back up to the higher level using the ladder to the right of the chest. You now have to fight some more enemies. There is a blue VIC cube up the stairs, so grab it if you want a power-up.

SHIP IN A BOTTLE

The third Ship in a Bottle is located to the right of the stairs at the far-right side of this area. Be sure to grab it and unlock some music for this world.

Don't miss the bombs in this area. They are great for blowing up crates or defeating enemies. To use a bomb, walk up next to a stack and press Use. Then press the Attack button to throw the bomb. If you don't throw it quick enough, the bomb blows up in your hands and you have to respawn.

COLLECTOR

Get all three of the Ships in a Bottle in this level in order to earn the Collector award.

Be sure to break open all the crates to collect all the Mickey coins, then head through the castle gate to exit the level.

Level 2

Start

- Collectibles: 3 Ships in a Bottle
- Friends to Rescue: 2

LEGEND

 Ship in a bottle   Star

 Challenge   Exit

VIC cube

BURN THE CARGO NETS

SHIP IN A BOTTLE

To the right of the cargo nets is the first Ship in a Bottle. Pick it up.

As soon as this level begins, move around smashing crates and picking up all of the Mickey coins you can find.

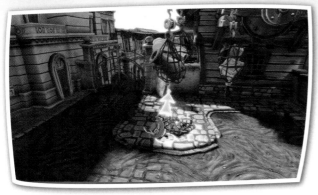

Walk over to the fire grate on the left side and hold down the Use button so you can move it. Position the fire underneath the cargo nets to burn the nets so a cannon barrel and crates drop down. Collect the coins from the crates.

BUILD THE CANNON

Drag the cannon barrel over to the gun carriage to assemble the cannon.

Challenge

After you build the cannon, an arcade game appears. Walk over to it and press the Use button to start a challenge.

CROSS THE GAP

Fight off any enemies that appear, then climb onto the cannon and drive it over to the right. Fire at the targets on the crate to break it open.

Climb up the stairs and push the levers on the spinning wheel to move the wooden bridge across the gap. Stop when it is in the middle and then walk across to get to the other side.

CLOSE THE BRIDGE

Walk down the steps to the green lever and press the Use button to move the lever and close the bridge. Flying Fodder appear, so hit them with a jump attack to knock them down.

Run across the bridge to pick up a blue VIC cube and use the Power-Up to help defeat the flocks of Flying Fodder that continue to attack you.

USE THE LIFT

Move to the left side of the bridge and climb onto the cannon. Drive it across the bridge. When an enemy hazard appears, blow it up with the cannon. You can also destroy hazards by attacking them with your tool.

Drive the cannon to the right and onto the lift. Then get off the cannon and use the green lever to operate the lift so you can get the cannon to the upper level.

BUILD THE LEVER

When the lift reaches the top, you must face a new enemy—a Brute. Rush toward the back of this area to pickup a blue VIC cube and use the Power-Up to help defeat the Brute.

Brute

Brutes are the lowest of the mini-bosses. They are larger than Fodder, can cause more damage, and are tougher to defeat. Brutes like to use ground slam attacks. When you see them jump up into the air, be ready to jump also to avoid the shock wave. The Brute gets stuck into the ground after a ground slam, so move in and attack before it can get up. Then move away and wait for another chance to attack.

If you are close by as the Brute begins its attack, a button icon appears over the Brute. Press the Use button to perform a counterattack that gets in some damage and stops the Brute's attack.

A star is suspended above a crocodile pit. Getting this star is tough. Move the fire grate in this area over by the cargo net. However, before setting fire to the cargo net, walk onto the red switch to close a hatch over the crocodile pit for a short amount of time. Now quickly set fire to the cargo net and move out onto the hatch to catch the star, then get off the hatch before the timer runs out. The star upgrades your tool.

Pick up the lever and carry it to the switch by the gate. Place it in the switch and then use the lever to open the gate. You will have to fight off several enemies in this area. There is a blue VIC cube here to help you with a Power-Up.

SHIP IN A BOTTLE

Walk up the steps to the right and get the Ship in a Bottle that is under a cargo net. Fight off any enemies that appear.

Try using the bombs on the right side of this area. Not only do they eliminate enemies, but also other players so you can move in to get the coins and other goodies.

EXIT THE LEVEL

SHIP IN A BOTTLE

You can find the third Ship in a Bottle below the spinning wheel. Be sure to pick it up before exiting the level. If you picked up all three in this level, you unlock some concept art that can be viewed from the main menu.

Turn the spinning wheel to move nearby objects.

As you near the green lever, it is taken up onto a round platform. Turn the spinning wheel to the right of the platform to lower it so you can get the lever.

Use the fire grate to burn the cargo nets in this area and collect the coins that come out. Then head through the portal to exit the level.

Level 3

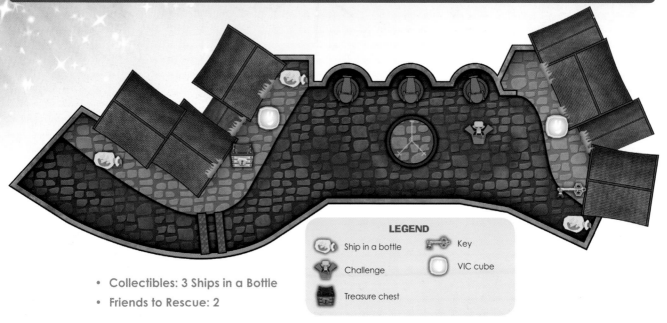

- Collectibles: 3 Ships in a Bottle
- Friends to Rescue: 2

LEGEND

 Ship in a bottle   Key

Challenge   VIC cube

Treasure chest

ENTER THE TOWN

As soon as you start this level, Fodder come to attack. Defeat them and collect all the Mickey coins.

SHIP IN A BOTTLE

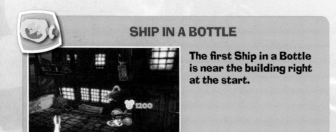

The first Ship in a Bottle is near the building right at the start.

Walk to the right. Enemy spike traps block your way into the town. Stand near them and then jump up and do a ground slam attack to destroy them. Then walk into the town.

DESTROY THE SHIP

Pirate ships have sailed up the Thames and are attacking London. This area is filled with enemies, including a Brute. Defeat all of these enemies. Blue VIC cubes are on the on the left and right sides by the burning buildings. Pick up one for a Power-Up.

SHIP IN A BOTTLE

A second Ship in a Bottle is near the cannon on the area's left side.

PUT THE FIRES OUT

As you are fighting against the enemies, a cannon trap appears and starts firing cannon balls at you. Move in close and attack its stand to destroy it.

Before you can attack the pirate ship, you have to put out the fires. Pick up water balloons from baskets near the buildings and throw the balloons at the buildings to put out the fires.

SHIP IN A BOTTLE

The third Ship in a Bottle is in the bottom-right corner of this area. Get all three in this level to unlock some character models.

SERIOUS COLLECTOR

Collect all nine collectibles in this location and you earn the Serious Collector award.

When playing with other players, rush across to the bottom-right corner of this area to find the key. Carry it over to the chest on the left side by the burning building and open the chest to get a star to upgrade your tool.

After you put out all of the fires, the pirate ship moves in to attack again. Take control of one of the cannons on the dock and fire away at the ship as it moves in to attack. The ship's damage meter at the bottom of the screen lets you know how close the ship is to sinking.

After the ship passes by, small boats approach. Fire at the targets on their sails to sink them.

If you did not destroy the ship, put out more fires and fight off Fodder who appear to attack you.

The pirate ship comes back, so open fire with the cannons again and sink it.

Challenge

An arcade game appears near the cannons as soon as you sink the pirate ship, providing a challenge for you to play.

FREE THE GUEST

After you have sunk the pirate ship, a guest wearing an Iago costume appears in the center of the area. Walk up to the guest to free him and unlock the Iago costume. You can now purchase it from the main menu.

After completing London once, play through the three levels again to free a second guest and unlock the Red Queen costume. When you replay a location, you often face more and tougher enemies. However, you also should have some upgraded tools.

Disney TRIVIA

The *Pirates of the Caribbean* movies are based on the popular attraction of the same name, which opened at Disneyland in California in 1967. The attraction was also built at the Magic Kingdom in Walt Disney World as well as Disneyland Paris and Disneyland Tokyo.

QUEEN ANNE'S REVENGE
Level 1

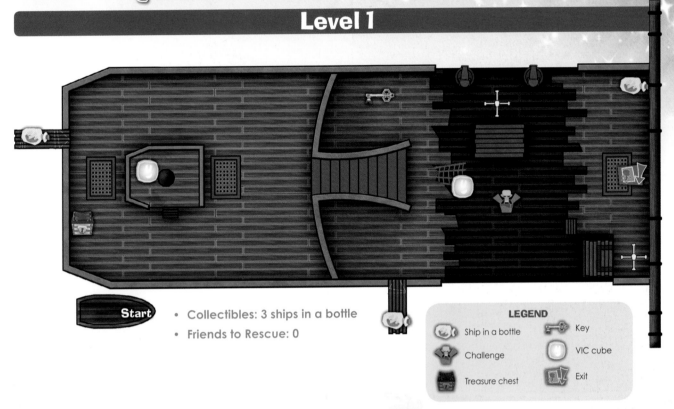

Start

- Collectibles: 3 ships in a bottle
- Friends to Rescue: 0

LEGEND

Ship in a bottle		Key	
Challenge		VIC cube	
Treasure chest		Exit	

Disney TRIVIA
There really was a pirate named Blackbeard. His real name was Edward Teach and the name of his ship really was the *Queen Anne's Revenge*.

USE TRITON'S SWORD

Now that you have completed the London levels, you are now on Blackbeard's ship, the *Queen Anne's Revenge*. Just like London, there are lots of enemies here to try to stop you from rescuing more guests.

Jump from the row boat onto the deck of the ship. Collect some Mickey coins that are here. Use the fire grate to burn a cargo net for more coins. Now head to the right side of this deck to pick up Triton's sword.

Triton's sword is magical and brings the ship to life. Look for ghostly images of the sword stuck into sockets on the ship. Place the sword into these sockets to activate different objects. You can take the sword out of a socket and use it again in other sockets.

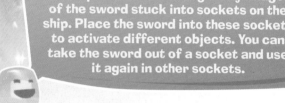

SHIP IN A BOTTLE

Carry Triton's sword to a socket next to a skeleton on the far-left side of the foredeck where you begin. Once you insert the sword into the socket, a plank extends from the deck, allowing you to walk along it to get the first ship in a bottle. Pull the sword out of the socket and continue on your way.

Triton's sword can be used to bring the ship to life!

Insert the sword into the socket near the row boat to lower a nearby ladder.

DISABLE THE SWORD TRAPS

Climb up the ladder to a small platform. Pull on the green lever to disable the sword traps blocking the way to the main deck.

As soon as you pull the lever, several enemies appear on the aft deck, including a Brute. Pick up the VIC cube on the platform and then drop down to the deck and begin fighting the enemies. Concentrate on the Brute first since it is the biggest threat. Use slam attacks as much as possible. If you are wearing the same costume as before, your tool should be upgraded and have special effects when preforming slam attacks. You must also use a slam attack to destroy a barrier that blocks your exit from the aft deck. You can also throw some bombs at the enemy—just be careful not to blow yourself up.

While other players are battling the enemies, climb up the ropes on the far side of the deck to collect lots of Mickey coins. It is a shame to let them go to waste—or to the other players.

USE TRITON'S SWORD

Make sure you have collected all the coins and hearts left behind by your defeated enemies, then pick up Triton's sword again and walk down the steps to the main deck. Drop the sword and fight some more enemies that appear, then pick up the sword again.

SHIP IN A BOTTLE

Place the sword into the socket by the side of the ship next to a skeleton and another plank extends from the ship. Walk out onto it to get the second ship in a bottle.

Before putting the sword into the socket in the middle of the deck, move the fire grate over to the cargo net and set it on fire. Pick up the key that drops out and carry it back up the stairs to open the chest on the aft deck to get a blue star to upgrade your tool.

Smash crates to find more coins and then find the wheel made of bones and move it over to the pulley by the cannons.

LOWER THE CRANE PLATFORM

Take Triton's sword and place it into the socket in the middle of the deck. This causes an explosion that destroys part of the deck, dropping you down to a lower deck as another pirate ship appears and begins attacking.

Now turn the wheel in a clockwise direction to lower a platform that you can use to get to the higher deck on the right.

BUILD THE WHEEL

As the pirate ship begins attacking, move over to one of the cannons and start firing at the ship. Get in some hits and it sails away. However, you now have to defeat a Brute. You can use Aa VIC cube and bombs along the left side of the lower deck to help you in your fight.

Challenge

After you lower the crane platform, an arcade game appears. Play this challenge to score some goodies.

JUMP ACROSS THE CRANE PLATFORM

Climb up the rope ladder on the left side. You can't take Triton's sword with you; however, you can come back for it later. As the crane platform moves toward the left side, jump onto the platform and ride it across. Jump off onto the deck on the right side.

SHIP IN A BOTTLE

Once you get to the right side, break up some crates near the side of the ship so that you can collect the third ship in a bottle and unlock some music.

LOWER THE LIFT

Now turn the wheel on this small deck in a clockwise direction to lower a lift with a socket on it.

Drop down to the lower deck and pick up the sword. Place it in the socket on the lift, then climb up the ladder to get back up to the deck on the right.

USE THE LIFT

Head back to the wheel and turn it in a counterclockwise direction to raise the lift and bring Triton's sword up to your level.

USE TRITON'S SWORD

Defeat any enemies that appear, then pick up Triton's sword and place it in the socket by the skeleton. This opens a hatch. Drop down into the hatch to exit this level and enter the next.

Level 2

LEGEND

- 🚢 Ship in a bottle
- 🗝️ Key
- ⚔️ Challenge
- ⬜ VIC cube
- 🧰 Treasure chest
- 📄 Exit

- Collectibles: 3 Ships in a Bottle
- Friends to Rescue: 0

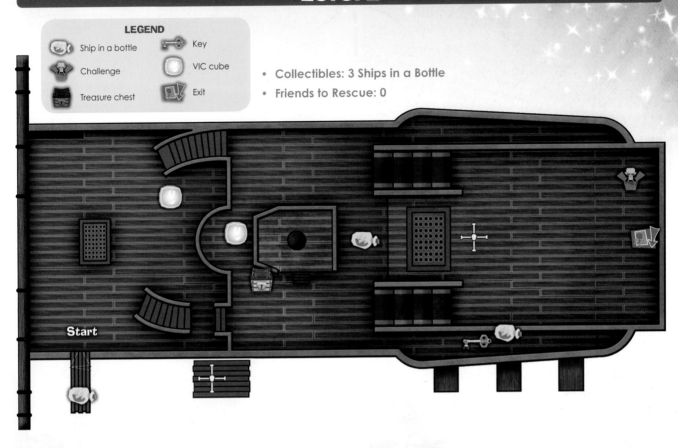

Start

USE TRITON'S SWORD

You emerge from a hatch on another deck and are immediately attacked by enemies. Fight them off. A VIC cube here can help with a power-up as well as some bombs.

Collect all the coins you can, then climb up the steps to pick up Triton's sword.

SHIP IN A BOTTLE

Place the sword in the socket by the skeleton, then walk out onto the plank to get the first ship in a bottle for this level.

![Disney Universe]

Carry the sword to the socket by the door and insert it to lower a ladder that leads up to another flight of steps.

GET TO THE NEXT DECK

Climb up the ladder and continue up the steps to a higher deck.

LOWER THE CRANE PLATFORM

Fight off a few enemies, then move over to the wheel and turn it in a clockwise direction to lower the platform. At the bottom, some spike traps block your way. Do a slam attack next to them to destroy them.

USE TRITON'S SWORD

Walk out onto the deck and defeat some more enemies. Then pick up the sword and place it in the socket on the crane platform. This extends some small platforms out from the side of the ship, which you can jump over to get some coins. Turn the wheel in a counterclockwise direction to raise the platform back up to the higher deck.

DISABLE THE SWORD TRAPS

Carry the sword over to the socket by the mast and insert it to lower a ladder. Then climb up the ladder to the small platform.

Pull the green lever on the platform to stop the sword traps from spinning around and blocking your way.

USE THE LIFT

Drop back down to the deck and place the sword in the socket by the side of the ship. This raises hatches that you can use to jump to the stern of the ship. Then jump back onto the side deck and collect coins as well as a key. Carry the key back to the chest by the mast to get a blue star to upgrade your tool.

Now take the sword to the socket by the disabled sword traps. After you insert it, the moving stairs start going up rather than down.

Ride the stairs to the top and then turn the wheel in a clockwise direction to raise a lift and bring Triton's sword up to the highest deck at the stern of the ship.

SHIP IN A BOTTLE

Move to the small platform by the socket with the sword in it and stand on the footprints. As the cage swings over you, press the use button to grab onto it and swing across to get the second ship in a bottle.

SHIP IN A BOTTLE

Jump over the railing on the upper deck and land on a canopy to find the third ship in a bottle. Get it to unlock some concept art.

Challenge

After using the lift to get the sword up to the highest deck, an arcade game appears in the deck's far-right corner. Use it to play a challenge.

USE TRITON'S SWORD

Place Triton's sword in the socket at the stern of the ship to open doors to the captain's cabin and the exit. Go through the exit to get to the next level.

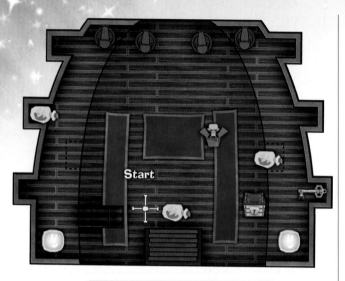

LEGEND

🍾	Ship in a bottle	🗝	Key
🛡	Challenge	◻	VIC cube
📦	Treasure chest		

- Collectibles: 3 ships in a bottle
- Friends to Rescue: 2

DISNEY TRIVIA

The name of the pirate ship attacking the Spanish fort in the Pirates of the Caribbean attraction at the Disney theme parks is the *Wicked Wench*.

BUILD THE WHEEL

You are now in Blackbeard's cabin and a pirate ship begins firing on you. Collect as many coins as you can at the start while dodging cannonballs. Then move to the left side and pull out some stairs.

Climb up the stairs and then pull on the green lever to open a cell and find the wheel. Drag the wheel down onto the main floor and place it in the correct position.

SHIP IN A BOTTLE

Pull the green lever next to the wheel's cell to open another cell, where you can pick up a ship in a bottle.

USE TRITON'S SWORD

Turn the wheel in a clockwise direction to raise a platform with Triton's sword on it. Pick up the sword and carry it to the socket in the middle of the floor. This opens four cells, each containing a cannon that slides out for you to use.

DESTROY THE SHIP

As the ship moves toward you, take control of a cannon and start firing. Hit the enemy cannons as they stick out of the hatches on the ship to cause damage to the enemy ship.

> After the large ship pass by, the deck of your ship tilts in one direction. Watch for sliding cannon and large round mines rolling about, which can hurt if they hit you.

The ship sails away for a bit, so fight off the enemies that appear and climb up the ladder to the upper-left side of the area. Pull on green levers to find a key to a treasure chest containing a blue star on the main floor. Also get a green lever from the other cell and carry it down to the main floor.

Down on the main floor, slam attack near the spike traps and barrier which appear, then fight off the enemies.

SHIP IN BOTTLE

Place the green lever in the switch on the right side and pull on it to open a cell holding the second ship in a bottle.

A Brute appears and attacks at the same time the pirate ship is firing cannon balls at you. Dodge the cannonballs and defeat the Brute with slam attacks as you dodge.

SHIP IN A BOTTLE

Climb back up onto the right walkway and stand on the footprint pad. Grab onto the cage as it swings by and ride it out over the main floor to get the final ship in a bottle and unlock some character models.

31

Once you have all the collectibles and coins, you must balance your time between fighting enemies that spawn in and attacking the pirate ship. It sends five small boats toward your ship. Hit the targets on their sails to destroy them. Then as the large ship closes, fire the cannons at the cannon ports until the ship sinks.

Challenge

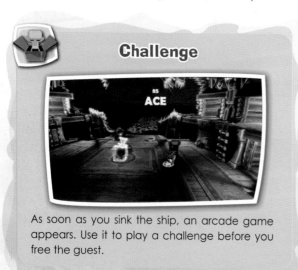

As soon as you sink the ship, an arcade game appears. Use it to play a challenge before you free the guest.

FREE THE GUEST

Now go over and free the guest to unlock the Quorra costume.

Play through the *Queen Anne's Revenge* again to free another guest and unlock the Minnie costume.

FOUNTAIN OF YOUTH
Level 1

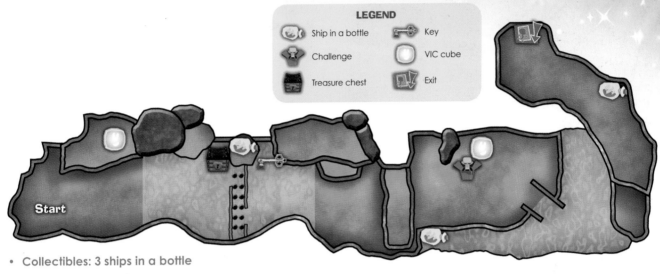

LEGEND

- Ship in a bottle
- Challenge
- Treasure chest
- Key
- VIC cube
- Exit

Start

- Collectibles: 3 ships in a bottle
- Guests to Rescue: 0

USE THE CURSED FIRE

This location takes place in a cavern where you must fight enemies and move through underwater areas to complete objectives. Collect the coins near the starting spot and use the VIC cube for a power-up to help defeat the enemies that attack.

As a zombie pirate, you can walk underwater. However, you can't jump or drive. To change back to your normally cheerful self, use the cursed fire again. Don't try to go into the water unless you are a zombie or you'll die.

While your fellow players are battling the enemies at the start, rush to the cursed fire and turn into a zombie. Then go into the water to collect all the coins you can before they get down there.

Walk up to the cursed fire and stand on the footprints. Press the Use button. The cursed fire transforms you into a zombie pirate.

Disney TRIVIA

Jack Sparrow was created for the first *Pirates of the Caribbean* movie, *The Curse of the Black Pearl*. He did not appear in the original attraction. However, after the release of the second movie, *Dead Man's Chest*, audio animatronic Jack Sparrows were placed into the attractions at the Disney theme parks, along with an audio animatronic Captain Barbossa and a projection of Davy Jones, that was later replaced by Blackbeard.

CROSS THE DEADLY WATER

As the zombie pirate, walk down into the water. Hit the coral around a wooden platform to cause it to float up so that you can get some coins. Then drop back down into the water. You next have to get past some spears that rise up from the sea floor. Hit the coral and wait for the spears to go past you toward the rear of the area. Now rush through the narrow passage and get to the right side before the spears start coming up in the opposite direction.

Once you get through the spears, grab the key and go back through the narrow passage to get to the chest. You get a blue star for upgrading your tool. Then head back through the spears once again and climb up onto the dry land and use the cursed fire to change back to your normal self.

Fight the enemies that appear on the shore and then use a slam attack to destroy the spike trap to the right.

SHIP IN A BOTTLE

After fighting the enemies on the shore, jump up onto the ledge at the rear of the area, then head to the left. Jump across to a rocky platform to get the first ship in a bottle in this level.

OPEN THE SPIKE GATE

Continue to the right and fight several enemies including a Brute. Rush to the VIC cube in this area and use the power-up to help defeat your foes.

You need a cannon, but the barrel is behind the spike gate. The lever to open the gate is underwater, so use the cursed fire and then head down into the water.

Move to the right and attack the coral to cause a wooden platform to float up to the surface. Get some coins.

Now walk to the left. Another row of spears rises up and drops down. As they move away from you, move forward and into the alcove with the green lever. Pull the lever to open the spike gate.

Challenge

After you open the statue doorway, an arcade game appears to the left. Use it to play a challenge either by yourself or against other players.

SHIP IN A BOTTLE

After pulling the lever, move to the left and cut down some coral so you can get to another alcove with a ship in a bottle inside.

SHIP IN A BOTTLE

Drive the cannon to the right side of this area and fire at the targets on door across the water. One of the doors has a ship in a bottle behind it. Collect this third bottle to unlock some music.

OPEN THE STATUE DOORWAY

Head back up onto land and use the cursed fire again. Back to your normal self, walk to the left and move the cannon barrel onto its carriage.

EXIT THE LEVEL

Walk to the right side of the area and jump across to the floating platform. Then jump again to the ledge on the right side.

Drive the cannon and fire at the targets to turn the wheel. Keep firing to open the statue doorway.

Head through the exit to go to the next level.

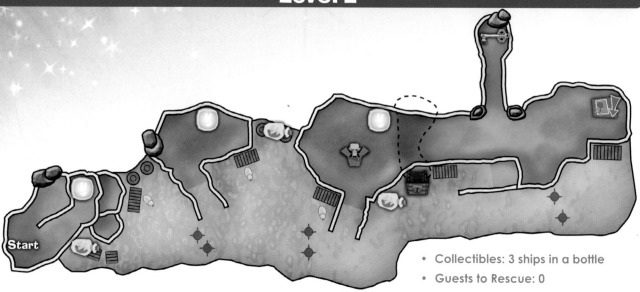

Start

- Collectibles: 3 ships in a bottle
- Guests to Rescue: 0

GET TO THE EDGE OF THE LAKE

At the start, move to the right and get ready to fight some enemies. Grab the VIC cube for a power-up to help you defeat the Fodder.

PASS BY THE FIRST MINES

Use the cursed fire to turn into a zombie pirate and then drop down into the water.

SHIP IN A BOTTLE

Walk along the bottom of the sea toward the left. Attack the coral and ride wooden platforms to the surface to get the first ship in a bottle.

Walk underwater to the right and pull the green lever to cause the two mines to rise up and clear a way for you to pass under them. Continue all the way to the far end of the level, collecting coins. Then return to where you first entered the water near the start. Pull levers on the way back to lower all the mines.

While you can get all the way to the far end as a zombie pirate, you'll miss out on some of the coins and other goodies. Once you get back, use the cursed fire to change back to normal and then walk out onto the dock and press the Use button to ride on the duck.

These ducks are like floating cannons. Shoot at the targets to flip over barrels so you can use them to jump across from land to land. Then sail over the first set of mines.

CONTINUE PAST THE NEXT MINES

Before disembarking on the dock in the next area, shoot at the targets on two more barrels to flip them over so that you can use them for jumping.

Move over to the dock and press the Use button to get off the duck. Now fight a Brute and several enemies. There is a VIC cube here if you need it.

SHIP IN A BOTTLE

Jump across the second set of barrels to collect the second ship in a bottle, which floats up in the air in between them.

RIDE THE DUCK UPSTREAM

In the next area, fight some more enemies and destroy the cannon trap. Once they are all defeated, pull on the green lever to retract some spears and clear the path to a ship in a bottle.

Challenge

After you pull the lever, an arcade game appears. Use it to play a challenge and collect some goodies.

SHIP IN A BOTTLE

Hop onto a duck and sail it over to the right to collect the third ship in a bottle where the spears used to guard it. This unlocks some concept art. Then blast the target on the door to open a passageway between land platforms.

SAIL PAST THE FINAL MINES

Fire the duck's cannon at a target on a gate. There is a key behind it. Also, watch out for the cannon trap. If you stay to the right of it, it won't fire at you.

Jump off the duck and go get the key along with some coins.

Carry the key to the closest cursed fire and set it down so you can change into a zombie. Then pick up the key and walk down into the water. At the bottom of the ramp, open the chest to get a blue star for upgrading your tool.

Climb back onto the land, use the cursed fire to return to normal, and ride a duck past the last pair of mines.

CLEAR THE STATUE DOORWAY

Fire the duck's cannon at the target on the wooden doorway to clear a path to the exit.

EXIT THE LEVEL

Now sail the duck to the dock and jump off. Move through the exit to get to the next level.

Level 3

LEGEND

- Ship in a bottle
- Challenge
- Treasure chest
- Key
- VIC cube

- Collectibles: 3 ships in a bottle
- Guests to Rescue: 2

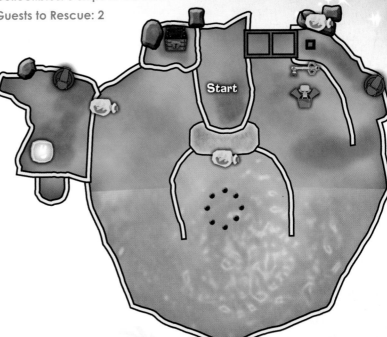

DISNEP TRIVIA

Johnny Depp modeled his portrayal of Jack Sparrow on Keith Richards from the music group the Rolling Stones. Keith Richards first appears in the third Pirates of the Caribbean movie, *At World's End*, playing the role of Jack Sparrow's father, Captain Teague.

ATTACK THE EVIL MERMAID

This last level of the location features a mermaid. To attack her, you first need to find a cannon barrel.

Start off by collecting coins and then dropping down to the lower area to the left.

Fight against several enemies that come to attack you.

SHIP IN A BOTTLE

Pick up bombs and throw them at the targets on the wooden doors to blow them open. A door underneath the cannon on the left has a ship in a bottle behind it. When the door is in splinters, get the bottle.

Use the cursed fire to turn into a zombie pirate, then walk down into the water. Pull on the green lever to lower the spears so that you can get to the cannon barrel.

SHIP IN A BOTTLE

Cut away the coral behind the spears so you can get to the second ship in a bottle hidden underneath the statue of a head.

Move the cannon barrel up the ramp on the right side of the level. Walk over the red switch to raise some platforms so that you can get across to the cannon carriage near the mermaid.

Use the nearby cursed fire to change back to normal and fight off any enemies that appear and attack. When they are defeated, use the cannon and fire at the mermaid to make her cry.

COLLECT THE MERMAID TEARS

As the mermaid cries, large teardrops fall to the ground. Quickly pick up a teardrop and carry it to the fountain. You can usually get three into the fountain before the rest disappear.

After collecting some tears, pick up a bomb on the right side and throw it at the nearby door with a target on it. Pick up the key inside and take it to the chest by the cannon you just built to get a blue star for upgrading your weapon.

Let the other players get the cannon barrel. While they are doing that, go after the key and the chest so you can get the blue star.

SHIP IN A BOTTLE

Pick up a bomb and quickly run up the ramp along the area's right side. Throw the bomb at the door next to the red switch. After the door is gone, collect the third ship in a bottle inside to unlock character models.

WORLD SET COMPLETE!
Earn this award by collecting all 27 world collectibles within a world. You can get this in the first world by making sure you get all of the ships in a bottle.

The mermaid fights back. She blows explosive kisses at you and sends shock waves that cause damage.

After crying, the mermaid moves to another spot. Use the cannon closest to her to fire and make her cry again.

Once again, pick up the teardrops and carry them to the fountain.

Fight off more enemies. VIC cubes are on both the left and right sides of the level. After the enemies are all defeated, fire a cannon at the mermaid again to get a final batch of teardrops. You need to get a total of eight teardrops to the fountain to complete this objective.

Challenge

After you get the last teardrop to the fountain, an arcade game appears to the right of the fountain. Play a challenge for some goodies and the pure joy of competition.

FREE THE GUEST

Make your way to the center cannon, where a guest is waiting for you to come and free him. When you do this, you unlock the Jack Sparrow costume.

Play this location again to free another guest and unlock the Blackbeard costume.

SWASHBUCKLER
By completing this final level of the *On Stranger Tides* world, you also earn this award.

FOUR STAR COSTUME
Earn this award by fully upgrading a costume. All it takes is collecting three blue stars while wearing the same costume.

ALICE WALKTHROUGH

WONDERLAND WOODS

Level 1

LEGEND

Drink Me bottle		Key	
Challenge		VIC cube	
Treasure chest		Exit	

- Collectibles: 3 drink me bottles
- Guests to Rescue: 0

Start

REBUILD THE STAIRCASE

As you begin your quest to rescue guests in the *Alice* world, you start off in the Wonderland Woods. Here you'll find different collectibles and items that you can use as you advance from level to level.

Once the enemies are gone, pick up the pocket watch near the middle of the area and place it in the socket next to the stairs to make them rise up.

UNLOCK THE GARDEN GATE

Climb up the stairs and hit a flower with a pocket watch in it to free the watch. Pick it up and then carry it down the stairs. Place it in the socket to open an alcove where you can get a key.

Flowers, mushroom, and other plants provide Mickey coins when you hit them with your tool. Collect some coins and fight off the enemies. Here they are dressed up as guards of the Red Queen.

> Pocket watches bring to life various things in Wonderland when placed into sockets. The pocket watches can be removed from sockets and used again in other sockets.

Carry the key up the stairs and use it to open the chest to get a blue star for upgrading your tool. Then head through the nearby door.

Ⓓⓘⓢⓝⓔⓨ TRIVIA

One of Walt Disney's first productions was a short called *Alice's Wonderland*. It featured a live-action girl in a world of cartoon characters. Filmed in 1923, Walt Disney would produce many more of these Alice comedies until the late 1920s.

The door takes you to another upper platform with a chess piece. Move the chess piece off the platform and place it onto one of the two round pads near the garden gate.

Move to the left side of the area and turn the wheel to fill the pond with more water.

Walk across some leaves to get to a platform in the pond, where a second chess piece is located. Move the chess piece across the leaves and to the second pad by the garden gate to open the gate.

DRINK ME BOTTLE

Before leaving this first area, step on this red switch; it makes a rock ledge extend from the rock wall. Then head up the stairs and go through the door to get to the platform where you found the first chess piece. From there, jump across to the ledge and then jump again to get the drink me bottle.

UNLOCK THE EXIT GATE

Grab a pocket watch from the first area and carry it into the second area so that you already have one to place into a socket right away.

This next area requires four chess pieces be moved onto pads in the center to unlock the gate. However, at the start, use a pocket watch to open alcoves along the right side to get some coins.

Walk up the stairs to get the first chess piece. Move it down the stairs and place it onto a pad.

Place pocket watches into the sockets near the back of the area to cause two containers to rise up. Climb up the stairs again and jump across these containers to get to a platform on the left side with another chess piece. Move it down to the ground level and place it on a pad.

Now place a pocket watch in the socket at the bottom of the platform from which you just dropped. This opens an alcove with the third chess piece. Move it onto one of the two remaining pads.

DRINK ME BOTTLE

While you are getting the chess piece on the back left platform, jump across to a couple of ledges to get a second drink me bottle.

Step on the red switch near the front-left corner of the area. The pond drains down to reveal another chess piece.

Challenge

After placing two chess pieces onto pads, an arcade game appears. Play a challenge to get some wonderful goodies.

As you try to drag the piece towards the pads, enemies attack. There are a couple VIC cubes in this area; use one if you need it to clear the area so you can continue with your objective.

As you are fighting enemies, watch for one enemy to build traps. An icon with a couple of gears appears, showing that a trap is being built. Attack the enemy to prevent the trap from being completed.

When all four chess pieces are on the pads, the exit gate opens. However, now you have to fight off more enemies as well as a Brute. This can be tough—especially if the enemy manages to get a cannon trap built. Move to one side where the cannon can't hit you and deal with the Brute first. Then finish off the rest.

DRINK ME BOTTLE

Before you exit the level, carry a pocket watch up the stairs and place it into the socket on the right side. This opens an alcove where you can get the third drink me bottle and unlock some music.

Head through the exit to end the level and start the next.

Level 2

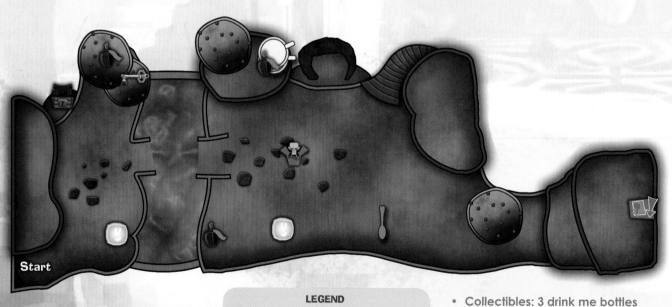

Start

LEGEND

Drink Me bottle		⚷ Key	
Challenge		◻ VIC cube	
▣ Treasure chest		Exit	

- Collectibles: 3 drink me bottles
- Guests to Rescue: 0

FIND AND USE THE HAT

Shortly after arriving at this level, enemies start attacking. Quickly defeat them or they can hurt you.

> There are bomb flowers in this level. Hit these flowers to release a bomb, then pick it up and throw it at the enemies—or at the other players and steal some of their coins.

After the enemies are defeated, move the hat located near the back of the area forward to where a ghostly image of it appears.

Jump in the hat to use it.

Jump into the hat and press the use button to fire yourself up to a ledge.

DRINK ME BOTTLE

Go through the door on the upper ledge. It takes you to a mushroom where you can get the first drink me bottle.

After getting the drink me bottle, drop down to a lower mushroom to get a key. Jump down to the ground and hit a bomb flower. Pick up the bomb and throw it at the target to blast open a door. Inside is a chest. Insert the key into the chest to get a blue star for upgrading your tool. Then use the hat again to jump up onto the ledge to get a pocket watch.

TURN BACK TIME

Place the pocket watch into a socket and a bridge appears. Cross the bridge to the other side of the level.

USE THE SPOON CATAPULT

A pocket watch is required.

Enemies attack you on the other side. Some also build spike traps in front of alcoves, so use slam attacks to destroy them.

Move the hat from the left side of the level to the right and place it just to the right of the bridge. Fire yourself up to a platform to get a pocket watch from a flower.

DRINK ME BOTTLE

Carry the pocket watch toward the front of the level and insert it into a socket to remove some vines and get the second drink me bottle.

DRINK ME BOTTLE

Move the spoon catapult by pushing it so that it targets the stack of cups by the hat. Jump up onto the handle of the spoon to launch a sugar cube at the cups. Launch more sugar cubes until the cups are all broken and a drink me bottle is revealed. Then jump into the hat and fire yourself up to get the bottle and unlock some concept art.

Move the spoon catapult's aim and use it to break open some alcoves and another stack of cups.

TAKE THE HAT TO THE RABBIT HOLE

As soon as you break the stack of cups on the right, enemies appear and start attacking. Plus you face a new boss—the Roto.

Roto

The Roto has one regular arm and one arm with a wrecking ball on the end. It has three different attacks. The Roto can thrust the ball at you, move around as it spins the ball low, or spin the ball up high in a larger circle. Don't try to attack the Roto while it is spinning or you will get hurt. Wait until after it finishes a high spin attack and is dizzy. Then move in and attack while it can't hit you back. Then when it starts spinning again, get out of the way.

Fight off the enemies and the Roto. Attack the smaller enemies while the Roto is spinning, then when it stops to recover, move in and get in a few hits with your tool.

 DIZZY!
Defeat a Roto to earn this award.

Move the hat up the stairs and along the path across the spider webs to the position at the bottom of a ledge.

EXIT THE LEVEL

Place two pocket watches in the sockets along the right side of the area to raise spider webs and create a walkway. Then put a third pocket watch in the socket near the stairs to raise them up as well and complete a path to the rabbit hole.

Jump into the hat and launch yourself up onto the ledge. Then go through the exit to get to the next level.

Disney TRIVIA

Walt Disney's full-length animated feature *Alice in Wonderland* was released in 1951. Tim Burton directed a live-action version of *Alice in Wonderland* for Disney, which was released in 2010.

Challenge

As soon as you insert the pocket watch into the socket near the stairs, an arcade game appears. Go over and use it to play a challenge.

Level 3

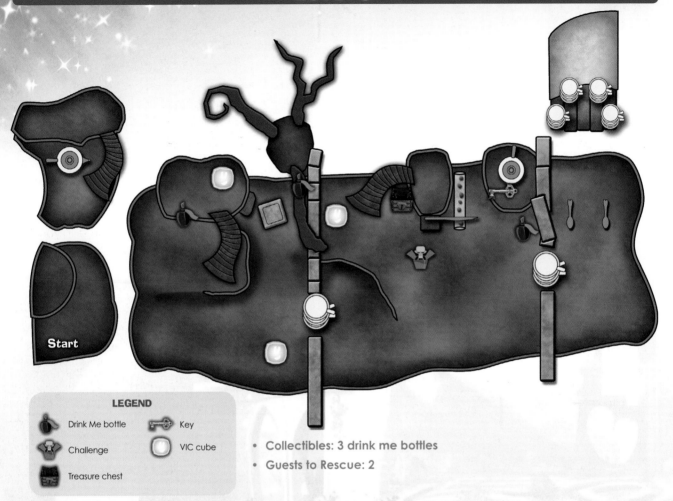

LEGEND

- Drink Me bottle
- Challenge
- Treasure chest
- Key
- VIC cube

- Collectibles: 3 drink me bottles
- Guests to Rescue: 2

OBTAIN THE CANDLE

To get the candle, you first need a pocket watch so you can move the vines blocking your way to it.

Jump across the gap to the right and step on the red switches to unroll the party horns. These act as bridges so you can move across the gap. Some enemies come to attack, so fight them off with your tool.

Now climb up the stairs and hit the flower to get a pocket watch. Pick it up and carry it back down the stairs.

DRINK ME BOTTLE

Place the pocket watch in the socket near the bottom of the stairs to open an alcove and get the drink me bottle hidden inside.

Set the pocket watch in the socket in the starting area to move the vines so you can get to the candle.

HEAT UP THE TEAPOT

Move the candle across both bridges and place it underneath the teapot to begin heating it up. When it boils, the spoon drops down to the ground.

DESTROY THE TEACUPS

Move the spoon across the bridge and take it to the salt shaker to the right to build a spoon catapult. Then take on the enemies that appear to try to stop you. Use the nearby VIC cube for a power-up.

DRINK ME BOTTLE

Go back and pick up the pocket watch and then place it in the socket under the tree limb on the right side to raise up a container. Then climb up the stairs and jump from the ledge across to the container and then on to the limb to get the second drink me bottle.

Walk back to the spoon and jump on the handle to launch sugar cubes at the teacups to break them and clear a way to the next area.

HEAT UP THE TEAPOT

Bring the pocket watch from the first area to save time in the second area.

As you enter the next area, be ready for a fight. Lots of enemies come and attack you. If possible, try to stop the Fodder who is building a cannon trap before it can complete the trap.

If you need to get a pocket watch here, jump up onto the cracker platform and move the knife back and forth to cut through the cake roll and release a pocket watch.

DRINK ME BOTTLE

Pull on the present to the right of the cake roll to open it and get the third drink me bottle and unlock some character models.

Place the pocket watch in the socket by the present to open an alcove and get a key. Then carry it over to the chest near the stairs to collect a blue star for upgrading your tool.

Now carry the pocket watch over to the stairs to raise them up.

Go to the candle near the entrance to this area and move it up the stairs. Step on the red switch at the top to unroll the party horn and take the candle across. Place it under the teapot to heat it up and get another spoon.

Challenge

As you step on the red switch by the party horn, an arcade game appears on the ground level. Use it to play a challenge.

DESTROY THE TEACUPS

Pull the spoon toward the salt shaker to build a spoon catapult. A Roto and several other enemies attack as you drop down to the ground. Keep your distance while the Roto is spinning and then move in for some hits while it is dizzy from spinning.

After defeating the enemies, jump on the handle of the spoon to launch sugar cubes at the teacups to destroy them.

RESCUE THE TRAPPED GUEST

Walk into the final area to find a couple of spoon catapults. Aim them and then jump on them to destroy four stacks of teacups. However, bombs come flying toward you so be sure to move away from them before the explode.

FREE THE GUEST

Once the teacups are destroyed, a stack of plates slide down. Walk across them to free the guest and unlock the Barbossa costume.

I captured another guest as well. Play through and complete Wonderland Woods a second time to unlock the Rafiki costume—if you can.

USE THE POCKET WATCHES

Pick up one of the pocket watches and carry it all the way to the entrance. Then follow a pathway that leads down to the other side of the pit. Place the pocket watch in the socket to complete the pathway to the right.

Now go back by the Bandersnatch and find the fire grate. Move it onto the lower pathway and use it to burn the cargo net and open a cage on the other side of the pit.

DRINK ME BOTTLE

Pull on the green lever to extend a walkway across the pit. Then step on the red switch on the left. This lifts the cage on the left and extends two small platforms. Move down the walkway and then jump across to the platform to get the second drink me bottle. Step on the switch inside the cell to make the platforms extend again if necessary and jump up out of the pit. Go back around and do the same thing again—this time stepping on the right red switch. Then go get the third drink me bottle and unlock some concept art.

As soon as you get one of the pocket watches out of the cage, pick it up and run to the pit to get the goodies while the other players are fighting against the enemies.

While in the cell on the right, pick up the key and make your way back around to the lever. Pull on it and walk all the way down the walkway to the chest and get a blue star for upgrading your tool. Then pull the lever to extend the walkway again so you can get back across.

Return to pick up the pocket watch. Then place the three pocket watches in the three sockets in the middle of the room.

Havi
must
varic
floati
mou
Step
amo

PLACE THE EYE IN THE PIPE

Climb up the stairs near the entrance and then jump across to the raised platform. From there, jump to a floating painting as it lowers down and then to another pillar and painting to finally get to a wooden platform.

Pick up the Bandersnatch eye and place it in the pipe. It rolls down and falls into the Bandersnatch's eye socket.

USE THE MONSTER'S TONGUE

Drop down from the platform and walk over to the Bandersnatch. Step onto its tongue. It flips you up onto the balcony.

EXIT THE LEVEL

Now walk through the blue exit to get to the next level.

Level 3

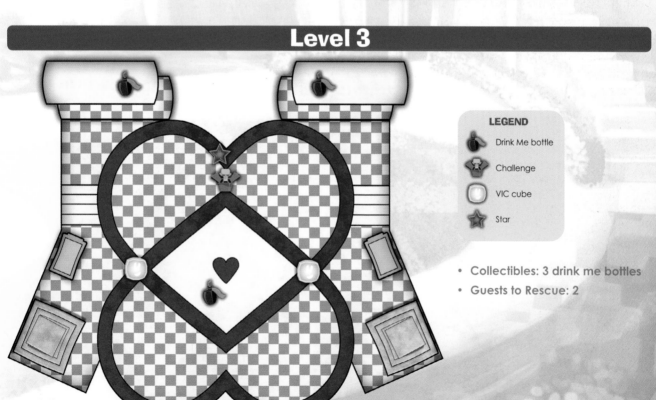

LEGEND

- Drink Me bottle
- Challenge
- VIC cube
- Star

- Collectibles: 3 drink me bottles
- Guests to Rescue: 2

COLLECT THE CARDS

This level takes place in a single room where you must collect cards. Not all of the cards are visible at the start. Pick up a card and then carry it to the heart-shaped table in the middle and place it on the stack.

If you thought it would easy to just pick up cards, you are wrong. Enemies start attacking, so you have to fight before you can continue collecting.

When playing against other players, you are competing to see who can get the most cards onto the table. Therefore, when the enemies start attacking, use that as the time to make a card rush and let the other players do the fighting for you.

After you get the first three cards to the stack, the Red Queen drops down on a platform and scatters three more cards before rising up again.

DRINK ME BOTTLE

The Red Queen also drops a drink me bottle near the table, so pick it up and add it to your collection.

The enemies like to build traps in this level. As you move about, be sure to destroy them with slam attacks and try to get rid of them before they are completed.

Two of the cards are on these checkered platforms at the far corners of the room. Take the back to the table. You can also find the hat on the left platform.

DRINK ME BOTTLE

Place the hat down on the pad and use it to get up to the higher platform, where the second drink me bottle awaits you.

After you have taken six cards to the table, the Red Queen returns and sends a Brute to attack you. Also, a sharp bar begins spinning around the table, making it dangerous just to carry the cards to the table. Defeat the enemies.

Move the hat to the far center of the floor and use it to shoot yourself into the air to get the blue star for upgrading your tool.

Don't forget to use bombs when facing Brutes and groups of other enemies. Use the VIC cubes in the area for power-ups.

DRINK ME BOTTLE

Now move the hat to the pad on the right side to get to the third drink me bottle and unlock some character models.

Collect three more cards. One is at the front and center of the room and the other two are on floating paintings over the side doors.

Want to stop other players from getting the drink me bottles on the high platforms? As they land on the platform, step on the red switch on the floor to send a wall of spikes smashing down on them. Then go and get it yourself before they can do the same to you!

DISNEY TRIVIA

The Alice world in Disney Universe is based on Tim Burton's version of *Alice in Wonderland*.

Pick up the watch at the back right side of the room and place it into a socket by one of the doors. This makes a platform rise up. Jump up onto the platform and then onto the painting to get the card. Once you have taken it to the table, move the pocket watch to the socket on the other side of the room and do the same thing again.

This time, when the Red Queen returns, she is firing lasers down at you. Dodge them and then collect three more cards. Two are up on the higher platforms; you need the hat to get to them.

After collecting 12 cards, you face more laser blasts and now two sharp bars are spinning around the table. Jump over them if you have to in order to avoid getting hit. Collect three more cards to complete this objective.

Challenge

After you get 15 cards onto the table, an arcade game appears in the back center of the room. Use it to play a challenge and score some coins.

FREE THE GUEST

Finally go and free the guest and unlock the Goofy costume while you are at it.

Complete this location again to free a second guest and unlock the CLU 2 costume.

INSIDE THE RED CASTLE
Level 1

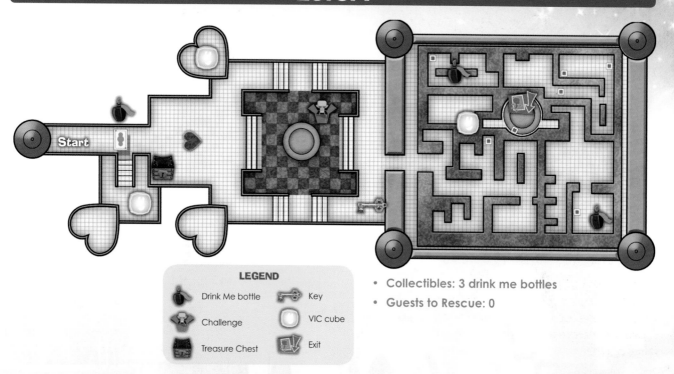

LEGEND

- Drink Me bottle
- Challenge
- Treasure Chest
- Key
- VIC cube
- Exit

- Collectibles: 3 drink me bottles
- Guests to Rescue: 0

FIND AND RETURN THE CARD SYMBOLS

This level takes place up on top of the castle. You need to find card symbols to continue. Start off by walking down the stairs to find a heart. Pick it up and walk back up the stairs.

Move quickly to the right; if you hurry, you can get to the pad in the middle of the grass before the enemies start attacking. Place the heart in the heart-shaped slot and then get ready to fight.

The Fodder try to build spike traps around the pad to prevent you from getting the symbols returned.

Use slam attacks to destroy the traps, then focus on defeating the Brute as well.

After the area is clear, pick up the spade, which is just to the right of the pad and carry it to the pad.

The diamond is on top of a tree. Move the hat to a spot next to the tree, then jump in and shoot yourself up onto the tree to get the diamond. Drop down and carry the diamond to the pad.

DRINK ME BOTTLE

Near where you began the level, jump across to a floating card and ride it around through the air to get the first drink me bottle. Then as the card returns near the wall, jump back onto the castle.

A key is hidden in the front-right corner behind some roses. Pick up the key and carry it to the chest to the left of the grassy square to get a blue star for upgrading your tool.

Now go pick up the club, which is near the chest. Carry it back to the pad.

Challenge

After you return the last symbol, an arcade game appears. Use it to play a challenge.

Once you have all four symbols in place, the golden gates to the right open. Walk through them into the next area.

FIND AND RETURN THE CLUB

You are now in a garden maze. The club is near the entrance. First off, fight the Fodder in this section of the maze to clear them out. You don't want them in the way since you have to move quickly.

Use bombs found in this area to blow up targets to release more coins or create openings in the hedges.

Bombs also work great for slowing down players who are trying to beat you.

DRINK ME BOTTLE

Jump into the hat and warp to an enclosed section of the maze. Watch out for the arrows in the sidewalk and, when it is clear, grab the drink me bottle in the middle.

Pick up the club and then move to the red switch. Watch the arrows popping up through the sidewalk to the right. As the arrows go down one side and start to go back up toward the gate, step on the switch and then move quickly to the gate, avoiding the arrows, and getting though before the gate closes. Place the club in the slot on the pad in the center of the maze.

FIND AND RETURN THE DIAMOND

Now walk over to the footprint pad and press the Use button to open the gate to another part of the maze.

Be sure to defeat any enemies between you and the pad. Then pick up the diamond and step on the switch.

Quickly jump into the hat, warp to the other hat, and rush through the gate to the pad before it closes. Place the diamond in the slot on the pad.

FIND AND RETURN THE HEART

Step on the footprint pad again and another gate opens. Move through it and pick up a bomb. Throw it at the target to the right to create a shortcut through the hedge. Then step on the red switch and hurry through the gate leading to the top-right corner of the maze. Pick up the heart, then step on the two red switches in this corner and rush all the way back to the central pad to deposit the heart in its slot.

FIND AND RETURN THE SPADE

As before, step on the footprint pad and go through a gate that leads to the lower-right corner of the maze. Get past a sidewalk with arrows and pick up a bomb. Throw it at the target so that you can get into the corner where the spade is.

DRINK ME BOTTLE

The third drink me bottle is next to the spade. Pick it up to unlock some music.

Move in and defeat the Fodder guarding the spade. Once you have picked up the spade, wait for the arrows in the sidewalk to move to the left past the entrance , then step on the red switch. Quickly move toward the gate leading to the center pad before the gate closes while avoiding the arrows.

EXIT THE LEVEL

After you have returned all four symbols to the central panel, the exit opens up. Walk into the blue center of the pad to enter the next level.

Level 2

LEGEND

- Drink Me bottle
- Challenge
- Treasure Chest
- Key
- VIC cube
- Exit

Start

- Collectibles: 3 drink me bottles
- Guests to Rescue: 0

FIND THE CLUB PIECE

At another location in the castle, you must once again find card symbols. However, instead of a maze, you have a track that you must manipulate. Right at the start you come under attack by enemies.

> While the other players fight the enemies, hit the tall patches of grass to find lots of coins for your collection.

DRINK ME BOTTLE

Hit the high grass along the left side of the area to cut it down. Not only do you find coins there, but also the first drink me bottle.

The club is on this platform on the area's right side. Pick it up and take it back to the slot in the center.

GET THE DIAMOND PIECE

After you place the club piece in the slot, the Red Queen pulls a lever and enemies appear. It is important to defeat them before continuing. Once they are defeated, step on the switch on the platform where you found the club to make a ball launch along the track.

Quickly move to the left side and step on the heart platform so that it is tilted to the right. Then, after the ball goes through the green heart on the far left, tilt the heart platform to the left to lower the section of track that the ball just passed and raise a section that it is approaching.

Now go to the heart platform at the front of the area. Tilt it to the right and then as the ball approaches the gap in the track, tilt is to the left.

When the ball reaches the end of the track, pick up the diamond released from the ball and carry it to the slot in the center. The Red Queen appears again and changes the track a bit.

GET THE HEART PIECE

More enemies appear, including a Brute. Defeat them all since you need this area clear. Experiment with using a couple of catapults since they modify the track for you.

DRINK ME BOTTLE

Take control of the catapult on the right. Aim it at the target by the Red Queen sign on the right. When you hit the target, a drink me bottle drops down. Pick it up.

Next aim at the target to the left by the track. Hit it to move a piece of track into place. Then hit the target to the right to fix another section of track.

Now take control of the catapult on the left. Aim at the target on a tall pillar and fire to knock of a key. Use the key to open a chest on the right side of the area and get a blue star for upgrading your tool.

You are now ready to launch the ball. Step on the switch on the platform. Now all you have to do is go to the heart platform at the front of the area and be ready to tilt it as the ball approaches the missing section. When it gets to the end, pick up the heart and carry it over to the slot in the center.

 ## Challenge

Now that three pieces are in position, an arcade machine appears. Use it to play a challenge to earn goodies and move up in the ranks against other players.

GET THE SPADE PIECE

More enemies, including a Roto, have been sent by the Red Queen to stop you from getting the last piece. Fight them off and clear the area before launching a ball.

The track is a bit different this time. Once again you have to tilt the heart platform on the left side. However, now you must step on red switches at three different locations to use jets of steam to push the ball over gaps in the track. Step on the switch on the platform to start the ball rolling. Then go to the switch at the far center of the area. When the ball is just about to the end of the track, step on the switch to activate the steam.

Tilt the heart platform on the left, then move down to the front area and step on two more red switches at just the right time to get the ball over the gaps. Pick up the spade and take it to the slot on the center to open the exit.

DRINK ME BOTTLE

Before going through the exit, launch the ball one more time. Do the same thing you did to get the spade by using the steam switches and the heart platform on the left. When the ball reaches the end, the drink me bottle inside is released for you to pick up.

Jump down into the exit to enter the last level of the Alice world.

Disney TRIVIA

In the battle scene in Tim Burton's version of *Alice in Wonderland*, the Red Queen's army is based on playing cards while the White Queen's army are based on chess pieces.

Level 3

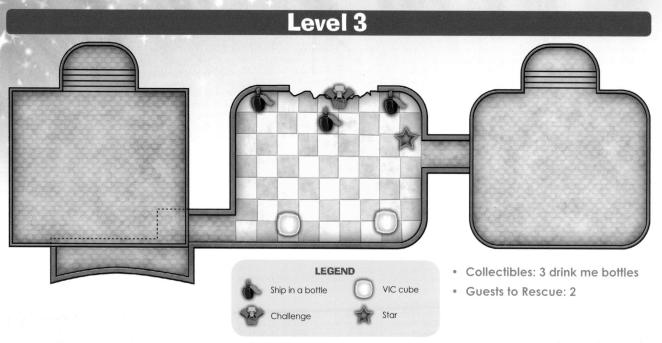

LEGEND

	Ship in a bottle		VIC cube
	Challenge		Star

- Collectibles: 3 drink me bottles
- Guests to Rescue: 2

FIND THE MONSTER

This final Alice level is a boss battle against the Jabberwocky. First you have to find it. Head to the right and get ready for a fight.

Start by fighting off several Fodder. There are some VIC cubes here for power-ups if you need them.

ATTACK THE MONSTER'S HANDS

The Jabberwocky finally makes its appearance. You must attack its hands. As it slams its hands down, jump over the shock waves to avoid taking damage and then slam attack its hands. You can also try throwing bombs at its hands to damage them.

After one of the hands is damaged, a target appears on it. Throw a bomb at the target to destroy the hand. If you don't hurry, the hand repairs itself and you have to attack it again and then blow up the target.

DRINK ME BOTTLE

After destroying one of the Jabberwocky's hands, a drink me bottle appears. Fight your way through the enemies to get to it.

ATTACK THE OTHER HAND

Now you have to destroy the Jabberwocky's other hand. Throw a bomb at it right away to damage it, then throw a bomb to destroy it completely. After the practice you had on the first hand, this one should go quicker.

DRINK ME BOTTLE

As soon as you destroy the second hand, pick up another drink me bottle.

Once again a bunch of enemies come to attack. Lay into them and clear the area so you can finish off the Jabberwocky.

DEFEAT THE MONSTER

For this final phase of the battle, targets appear on the monster's arms. Throw bombs and blow up each target.

The Jabberwocky has some deadly attacks. In addition to the shock waves, it also breathes fire at you. Jump out of the way or you will be hurt.

Once you destroy the two targets, the Jabberwocky falls down stunned. You need to hit it some more in the head.

When you cause enough damage, the monster opens its mouth and reveals a target. Throw a bomb at the target and destroy it to finally defeat the Jabberwocky.

DRINK ME BOTTLE

As the Jabberwocky falls from the walls of the castle, it leaves behind the last drink me bottle. Pick it up and unlock some character models.

Challenge

An arcade game appears as soon as the Jabberwocky is defeated. Use the game to play a challenge.

FREE THE GUEST

Now all that remains is to walk up and free the guest. For a reward, you unlock the Alice costume.

Play through this level again to rescue another guest and unlock the Mad Hatter costume.

TIME FOR TEA!
Complete the Alice world to earn this award.

Disney TRIVIA

Proper names were created for the characters in Tim Burton's version of Alice in Wonderland since the book and previous movies refer to characters other than Alice only by their descriptions. For example, the Caterpillar is named Absolem and Tarrant Hightopp is the name of the Mad Hatter.

LION KING WALKTHROUGH

LOWER PRIDE ROCK
Level 1

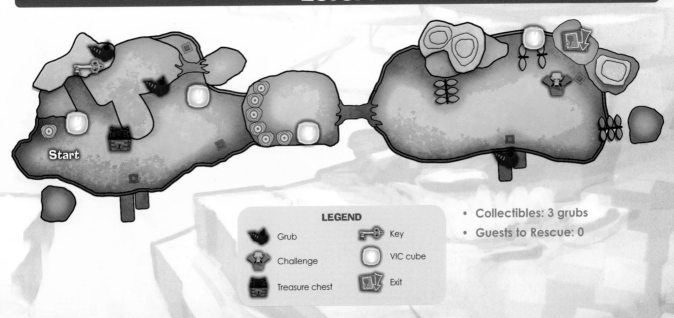

Start

LEGEND

- Grub
- Challenge
- Treasure chest
- Key
- VIC cube
- Exit

- Collectibles: 3 grubs
- Guests to Rescue: 0

BREAK THE ROCKS

You have now entered the world of *The Lion King*. The skills you have learned in previous worlds will help you survive. In addition, you must learn some new skills in this land of survival of the fittest.

At the start, gather some coins that are lying around. Hit plants to release some more coins. Then you have to deal with some Fodder as they attack.

> Look for red switches at the front edge of the area. Step on them to make ledges extend out from the cliff side. Drop down onto the ledges to get some coins, but be careful to jump back up before the timer runs out or you'll fall when the ledges retract.

Climb up the stone ramp to find some bombs. Also up in this area is a key. Pick it up and take it down to the chest at the bottom of the ramp to get a blue star to upgrade your tool.

GRUB

> While you are up by the piles of bombs, throw a bomb at the rock near the key. Once it is gravel, jump up and get your first grub.

Pick up a bomb and throw it at the rock on the other side of the cage. A red switch lies underneath the rock. Step on the switch to open the cage below.

> Throw a bomb at the tree to the right of the pile of bombs. Walk across on the trunk and find a drum. Drums in the *Lion King* world work like hats in the Alice world. Move it down to the ground and place it under columns of coins so you can shoot yourself up to get all of them.

Inside the cage is a cannon. However, before you use it, fight off some enemies that appear after you step on the switch. Once they are defeated, use the cannon to blast the row of rocks blocking the way to the right.

76

GRUB

A red switch is under the tree you can knock down with a bomb. Step on this switch to open a cage to the left. Inside, get the second grub. Yummmm!

KNOCK DOWN THE TREE

After blowing up the rocks, jump up to the next area. Now pick up a bomb and throw it at the tree to the right. The bomb knocks the tree down so you can continue moving to the last area to the right.

PLANT AND WATER THE SEEDS

Walk across the trunk of the tree and pick up a seed from a tree. Carry it to the right.

More enemies attack, so fight them off. Then pick up the seed if you dropped it and walk over to one of the holes. Press the use button to plant the seed.

Once you have planted a seed, throw a water balloon at it to make it grow into a tree. Plant a second seed next to the first and water it to create steps leading up to the exit.

As the second seed is growing, more enemies show up, including a Roto. Focus on the Roto first, staying out of its way and waiting for when it is dizzy to make your attack.

Challenge

After you plant the second seed to make the stairs to the exit, an arcade game appears. Be sure to use it to play a challenge.

There are two other spots where you can plant seeds and grow trees that let you get to coins and other goodies. While the other players are planting the seeds for the exit or fighting enemies, go after the goodies with a little planting of your own.

GRUB

Step on the red switch near the pile of bombs; a ledge will extend out from the cliff side. Drop down to the ledge to get the third grub and unlock some music.

EXIT THE LEVEL

Once you have all the goodies, jump up onto the leaves of the trees you planted to get to the blue exit. Go through it to continue to the next level.

Level 2

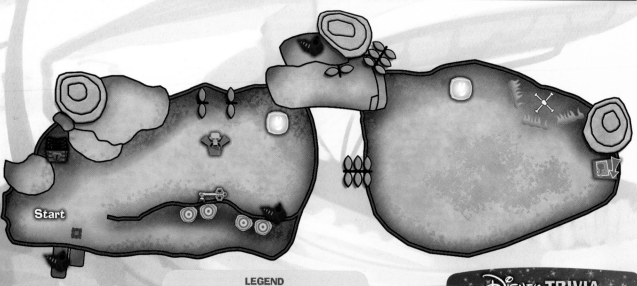

Start

- Collectibles: 3 grubs
- Guests to Rescue: 0

LEGEND

Grub		Key	
Challenge		VIC cube	
Treasure chest		Exit	

Disney TRIVIA

Released in 1994, *The Lion King* is Disney's 32nd animated feature.

GROW THE PLANTS

Once again, take some time at the start to collect coins and fight against enemies that seem to enjoy attacking you.

Pick up another seed and plant it next to the first. As you do this, lots of enemies attack. Be sure to use the VIC cube in this area for a power-up to help you out. When the enemies are defeated, throw water balloons at the seeds.

GRUB

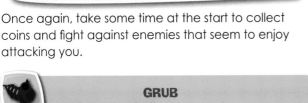

Step on the red switch near the pile of bombs and then drop down to the ledge to get your first grub of the level.

Challenge

After you water the two seeds you planted, an arcade game appears. Use this machine to play a challenge and earn some coins.

Throw bombs at the three rocks with targets on them. Now you can jump up the steps to get to the tree with the seeds.

Drop down to the ground to the right and plant the seed. Slam attack the spike trap nearby so that you don't step on it by accident during the fight with a Roto that appears. Use the same tactics against it that have worked in the past.

There are several rocks with targets on them on a lower pathway at the front of the area. Throw a bomb at the two rocks on the left to get a key that you can use to open the chest and get a blue star to upgrade your tool.

GRUB

A second grub is behind the two rocks to the right of the key. Use another bomb to blow up the rocks and then get the grub.

BUILD THE CRANK

Climb up the steps to get to the tree with the seeds. From there, jump across on the leaves of the two trees you just planted to get to the level's right side.

When you get to the other side, keep going to the right and pick up the VIC cube to help you deal with the enemies that attack.

GRUB

Pick up a seed from the tree and plant it near the rocky platform where you can see a grub. Water the seed and, after it grows, jump up on the leaves to get the third grub and unlock some concept art.

Plant some other seeds so you can get at some high-value coins.

Now use the water balloons to put out the fire. It is a good idea to put it all out. Then get the crank and move it into the position near the front of the level.

USE THE CRANK

As soon as you put the crank where it needs to go, several Fodder attack. Finish them off and then turn the crank in a clockwise direction to lower a cage and open the exit.

EXIT THE LEVEL

Now head through the exit so you can get to the next level.

Level 3

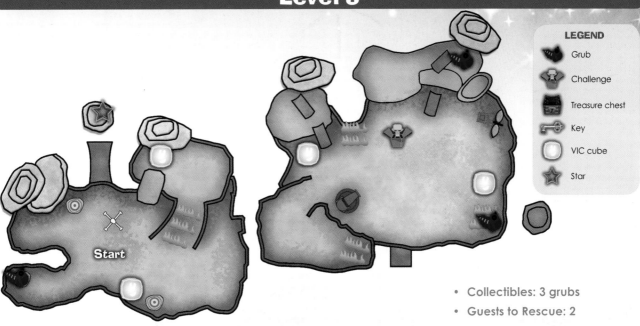

LEGEND

Grub	
Challenge	
Treasure chest	
Key	
VIC cube	
Star	

Start

- Collectibles: 3 grubs
- Guests to Rescue: 2

BUILD THE CRANK

GRUB

Pick up a bomb and throw it at the rock next to the crank. After it blows up, pick up the grub that was hiding behind the rock.

Use a bomb to blow up a rock to the left of the crank and step on the red switch underneath. Now walk out on a pathway to get to a blue star that upgrades your tool.

PUT OUT THE FIRES

Throw water balloons at the fire so you can get up the ramp and continue.

Move the crank to the spot near the cage and turn it in a clockwise direction to open the cage so that you can get to the water balloons. You also have to fight off lots of enemies that attack, including a Brute. Don't forget about the bombs. They work great against enemies and rocks alike.

KNOCK DOWN THE TREE

Climb up the ramp once the fire is out. Pick up a bomb and throw it at the tree to knock it down and create a bridge to the area to the right.

FIND AND PLANT THE SEEDS

Pick up the VIC cube and then race across the tree to get into a fight in the other side with your power-up already activated.

Once the enemies are defeated, put out the fires under the seed tree using water balloons. You can't get to the seeds until the flames are gone.

Pick up a seed and carry it to the right to plant it in a hole next to a platform.

GET THE CANNON PART

Water the seed with a water balloon to make it grow. The tree pushes on the platform and knocks the cannon onto the ground.

FIND AND BUILD THE CRANK

After the tree grows, a Roto and several Fodder attack. Use bombs and the VIC cube to help you defeat them all so that you can continue working toward the next objective.

Move the cannon barrel over to the turret and use it to fire at the target on the left. This destroys the chutes that drop rocks down from above. Shoot the other target to the right to prevent rocks from falling there as well.

Challenge

As soon as you destroy the targets to prevent the rocks from falling, an arcade game appears. Use it to play a challenge and score some coins.

GRUB

Throw a water balloon at the flames on the far right of the area so you can get the second grub.

Jump up onto the platform on the left to get the crank. Move it into the spot near the middle platform.

LOWER THE CAGE

Turn the crank in a clockwise direction to lower the cage holding the captured guest.

FREE THE GUEST

GRUB

Use the cannon to shoot at the rock on top of the middle platform. After destroying it, jump up onto the platform to get the third grub and unlock some character models.

Now move to free the guest and unlock the White Rabbit costume.

Play through this level a second time to free another guest and unlock the Sushi Chef costume.

ELEPHANT GRAVEYARD

Level 1

Start

- Collectibles: 3 grubs
- Guests to Rescue: 0

LEGEND

Grub	Key
Challenge	VIC cube
Treasure chest	Exit

EXPLORE THE AREA

The elephant graveyard is quite different from the previous level. Look for geysers that can propel you into the air to reach high places. As you step on the bones to the right of the start, you trigger geysers. Jump up onto the round rocks and ride them up to get lots of coins.

As you get down to the bottom of the bone steps, you have a fight on your hands. Enemies appear all around you. Take the time to defeat them, then focus on your objectives.

WATER THE PLANT

Some water balloons are in the front-left corner of the area. Pick one up and throw it at the nearby seed to grow a tree.

BUILD THE CANNON

Jump up onto the leaves of the tree, and then up to the platform. Move the cannon barrel down to the ground and then onto the cannon carriage.

BUILD THE LEVER

Hop onto the cannon and drive it to the left. Fire at the door with the target on it to blow it up. Inside is a lever.

Now drive the cannon to the right and blow up the barrier. Pick up the lever and use it to open a door with water balloons behind it. As soon as you pull the lever, a Brute appears. Defeat this enemy and then continue meeting your objectives.

Challenge

Pulling the lever also makes an arcade game appear. Be sure to play a challenge for some extra coins and glory.

WATER THE PLANT

Use the water balloons to water the seed so that you have a way to get to the next area. Also water a seed near the back of the area. Jump up onto the leaves and then to a platform to get a key. Take it to the chest over by where you got the cannon barrel and open it to get a blue star for upgrading your tool.

GRUB

On the same platform as the key, be sure to pick up the first grub.

GRUB

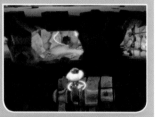

Before leaving the first area, move to the near-right corner and drop down onto a walkway. Step on a red switch to start a platform moving back and forth. Jump onto the platform and ride it past some cages. Use slam attacks to break open the cages. Inside of one is a grub. Get it and then ride the platform back to the right.

Now jump up onto the plant on the right to get up to the higher area.

BUILD THE CANNON

Fight off the enemies here and then drag the cannon barrel to the turret on the left side.

BUILD THE LEVERS

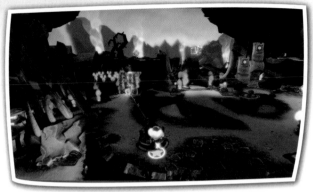

Fire the cannon at the door with a target on it so you can get to the lever inside.

Now pick up the lever and carry it over to the footprint pad. Use the lever to begin to open the exit.

Look for seeds lying in the ground. Some have nothing above them. However, if you water them, they grow and several coins appear above them.

Locate a second cannon barrel along the right side of this area. Drag it over to the second turret and get ready for some shooting.

Fire at the targets on some stone pillars. As you hit them, they tilt and form steps.

Climb up the steps and get the lever, then bring it back to put it in the slot by the second footprint pad. As soon as you do, be ready to fight more enemies. Some will try to build cannon traps next to the levers.

LIFT THE SKULL

GRUB

Step on the red switch near the front of this area. Then drop down onto some ledges that extend from the cliff side. Collect the third grub to unlock some music.

Now pull the levers if you have not done so already to lift the skull and reveal the exit.

EXIT THE LEVEL

Finally, move into the exit and get ready to begin the next level.

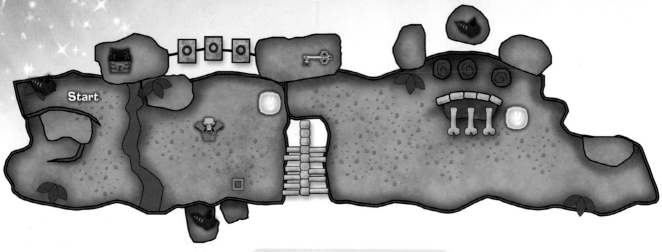

Start

LEGEND

Grub		Key	
Challenge		VIC cube	
Treasure chest		Exit	

- Collectibles: 3 grubs
- Guests to Rescue: 0

CREATE A CANNON

GRUB

Start off the level by getting your first grub. Throw a water balloon at the seed in the far-left corner. Then jump up onto the leaves of the plant so that you can get to the grub.

Drag the cannon barrel down from the platform and to the near-right corner and place it on the carriage. Then get ready to shoot.

Throw another water balloon at a seed on the center platform. Fight off all the enemies that attack and then jump up onto the plant so you can get to the cannon barrel at the top of the platform.

GRUB

Step on the red switch next to the cannon, then jump down to a couple of ledges to get the second grub.

BUILD THE BRIDGE

Fire at the three targets lined up in a row. As you hit them, they swing around to form a bridge. While you are on the cannon, go ahead and shoot the other targets you can see.

Challenge

As soon as the bridge is completed, an arcade machine appears. Use it to play a challenge. However, be sure to first deal with the enemies that also appear.

FIND THE BONE KEYS

Climb up to the platform where you got the cannon barrel, then jump across the bridge to get to another platform on the right. Pull the lever on the other side to open a door below so that you can get to some water balloons.

There is a key next to the lever. Pick it up and then jump back across the bridge to the chest where you can get a blue star to upgrade your tool.

Throw a water balloon at a seed to the right of the basket of balloons. Then jump up onto the tree. Jump up to a platform to get the first bone key.

Move the bone key into position next to another bone key and then fight the enemies that appear and attack you. A VIC cube is in this area, so use it for a power-up.

Drive the cannon to the right and shoot a target to lower a small platform. Use it to jump up to a stone ledge to get another bone key. Move the bone key back to where the other two are.

Now jump onto one of the bone keys, and then jump onto the other two. Stone platforms rise up, providing steps to get to the exit.

USE THE ORGAN

A Brute and lots of other enemies appear as soon as you place the last bone key. Fight them off to clear the area.

EXIT THE LEVEL

GRUB

Jump up the stone steps to get to the top. However, before you go through the exit, jump over to a platform to the left and get the third grub to unlock concept art.

Once you have the grub, move into the exit and advance to the next level.

DISNEY TRIVIA

The Lion King was the first Disney animated feature dubbed into the Zulu language.

Level 3

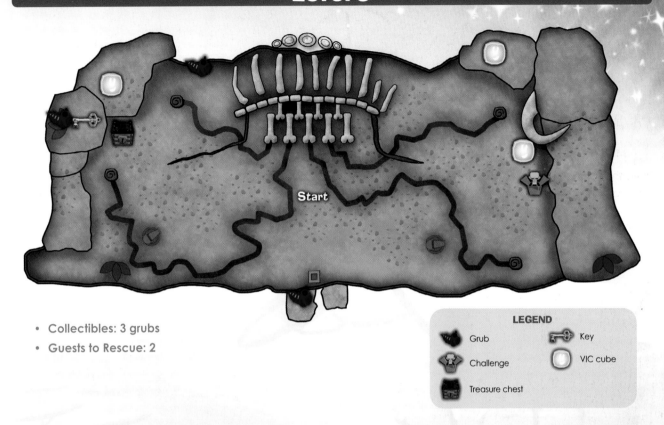

- Collectibles: 3 grubs
- Guests to Rescue: 2

LEGEND

Grub		Key	
Challenge		VIC cube	
Treasure chest			

PRESS THE FIRST ORGAN KEY

GRUB

Step on the red switch near where you start, then jump down to a ledge where you can find the first grub.

Now jump up onto the first organ key. This releases steam that travels through a pipe leading to a geyser.

RIDE THE ORGAN GEYSER

Quickly follow the lines from the first organ key to a round platform. Jump up onto the platform. A short time later, a geyser propels you up. Jump over to the adjacent ledge.

RETURN THE SECOND ORGAN KEY

As you land on the ledge, enemies appear and attack. Fight them off and then move the organ key off the ledge.

Move the organ key over to the organ and place it next to the first key.

Remember to water seeds to get lots of coins.

RECOVER THE THIRD ORGAN KEY

Step on the second organ key and then follow the line to another geyser on the left side. Ride it up to a ledge to find another bone key. Move it back to the organ and place it next to the second key.

GRUB

While next to the third organ key on the ledge, pick up a water balloon and jump up to a higher ledge to water a seed. After a tree grows, a grub appears. Jump up onto the tree to collect it.

Be sure to get the key that is next to the grub tree. Carry it down to the chest to get a blue star and upgrade your tool.

RETRIEVE THE FOURTH ORGAN KEY

GRUB

Use the cannon to shoot at the target at the area's far-left edge. This causes a ledge with a grub to drop down. Move to the ledge and collect the third grub to unlock character models.

Step onto the third organ key and then follow the line to a geyser in the front-right corner of the area. Ride it up to get a cannon barrel. Move the barrel down to the ground level and place it on the carriage before fighting off the mass of enemies that arrives to attack you. Also destroy any cannon traps the enemy builds.

Climb onto the cannon and fire at the three targets on the doors to the right. Inside is the fourth organ key. Move it to the organ.

> The cannon also can be used to attack enemies—or other players. The number of times you respawn affects your ranking in a game. Therefore, if you can cause other players to respawn more, you achieve a better rank.

Challenge

An arcade game appears after you blast open the doors with the targets on them. Use it to play a challenge either by yourself or against other players.

REPLACE THE LAST ORGAN KEY

Step on the fourth organ key, then follow the line to the last geyser. The enemies attack you here, but a VIC cube's power-up helps you get the job done. Move the last organ key to the organ and put it into position next to the other keys.

PRESS ALL OF THE KEYS

After the last key is in position, a brute and several other enemies appear. Move to a spot where you have some room to maneuver so you can dodge the Brute's attacks.

After the area is clear of enemies, jump on each of the five organ keys one at a time. The guest who is suspended up in the air drops to the ground.

FREE THE GUEST

Finally, walk up to free the guest and unlock the Nemo costume.

Complete this level a second time to free another guest and unlock the Baloo costume.

UPPER PRIDE ROCK
Level 1

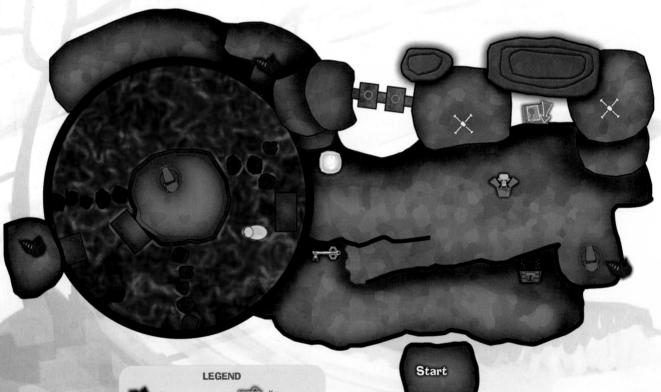

Start

LEGEND

- Grub
- Challenge
- Treasure chest
- Key
- VIC cube
- Exit

- Collectibles: 3 grubs
- Guests to Rescue: 0

USE THE PLUG

This location is filled with lava and other dangers. At the start, jump over to the main area from your platform and pick up the plug to stop the lava flowing along the ramp.

Remove the plug from the lava geyser on the left side to open a cave with a key inside. Take the key to the right side and open the chest to get a blue star for upgrading your tool. Be ready to fight off some enemies. Once you clear out the Fodder, head up the ramp.

RIDE THE DUCK

Walk to the left until you reach a lake of lava. Climb aboard the duck and set sail.

Fire the duck's cannon at targets on rocks as well as at rocks that block your path to the left side of the lake. You can also fire at the enemies on the island in the middle to clear it off before you land.

GRUB

Stop at the dock on the far left side of the area and get off. Jump up onto the top of the ledge and collect the first grub. Then sail the duck over to the island.

DEFEAT THE HYENAS

Take control of the cannon and shoot at the hyena targets as they move across the shooting range. You need to hit 20 hyenas to complete this objective.

GRUB

While you are on the duck, be sure to hit the target on the lake's far-right side. You have to fire across the island to hit it. When it's hit, the target flips over a rock, creating a platform in the lava. Now you can jump from the island to a ledge on the side of the lake of lava using this platform and get a second grub.

LOCATE THE CANNON BARREL

Sail the duck back to the shore and then climb up the wide steps leading to a bridge.

Jump across the bridge and turn the crank to lower a stone door and reveal the cannon barrel inside.

Challenge

After the door to the cannon barrel is opened, the arcade machine appears and is available for playing a challenge.

OPEN THE EXIT

Move the cannon barrel over to the turret and then fire at the target on the rocks. As one target is hit, another appears. Keep firing until you have carved a series of steps into the rock.

Climb up the steps and turn the crank to lower a lion door and open the exit.

EXIT THE LEVEL

GRUB

Go back to the cannon and fire at the target near the lava flow. As the lava adds weight on one end of this crane, the other rises, bringing a grub up with it. Grab it to unlock music.

Finally, walk into the exit to continue to the next level.

Level 2

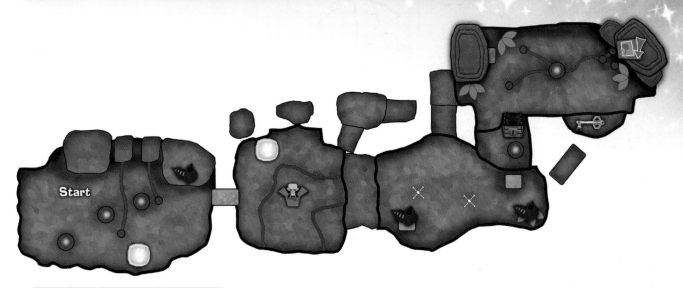

LEGEND

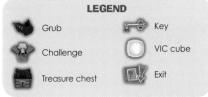

Grub		Key	
Challenge		VIC cube	
Treasure chest		Exit	

- Collectibles: 3 grubs
- Guests to Rescue: 0

DISNEY **TRIVIA**

Many of the names of the characters in *The Lion King* are Swahili words.

LOWER THE BRIDGE

Right at the start, go for the VIC cube and get the power-up so that you are ready to fight the enemies who appear.

Once it is clear, pick up the plug and place it on top of the lava geyser on the left side so that the lava is redirected down a channel to lift an elevator platform.

GRUB

Pick up a bomb and throw it at the rock with the target on it. After it blows up, get the grub that was hiding on the other side.

Ride the elevator platform up to the top to find the crank. Move the crank onto the elevator and ride it down. Move the crank across to the elevator platform on the right and leave it there.

PLUG THE GEYSERS

Fight off the enemies that attack you as soon as you cross the bridge. Watch out for a cannon that the Fodder like to build.

Remove the plug and then put it on the lava geyser to the right to send the flow toward the other elevator platform. Walk onto the platform and ride it to the top.

Pick up a bomb and move close to the stone slab with a target on it. Throw it at the target to open an alcove. However, lava is flowing over the entrance.

Move the crank off the elevator at the top and into its position. Then turn it to lower the bridge so that you can get to the right side of the level. Get down to the ground and then walk across the bridge.

Step on the red switch to temporarily stop the lava flow. Rush into the alcove, pick up a plug, and then get out.

Place the plug on one of the lava geysers. Then go get the plug from the previous area and place it on the second lava geyser. This clears away the wall of bubbling lava that blocked your progress.

As soon as you put the crank is position, a Brute appears. Give yourself some space to move around and then fight until you defeat this enemy.

Challenge

As soon as you plug the second geyser, the arcade machine appears. Use it to play a challenge.

DIRECT THE LAVA

Jump over the lava ditch and then move toward the back of the area to get a crank. Wait until an elevator platform rises, then move across. Let it go down and when the platform comes back up, move the crank across and place it in its slot.

GRUB

Turn the crank on the left so that the flow goes down to a small stone platform. Pull the green lever to send lava into the channel and then jump onto the platform. The lava raises it up so you can jump up and get the second grub.

Move to the right of the two cranks and pull on another green lever. This raises a platform that leads to a cave with a key. Jump across to get the key and then hurry back before the platform drops down into the lava. Place the key on the small platform by the lever.

GRUB

Pick up a water balloon and throw it at the seed by the lever. When the tree grows, jump up onto its leaves to get the third grub and unlock concept art.

Now turn both cranks so that the flow goes from the left crank to the right crank and then on to another platform. Pull the green handle by the left crank and then hurry back to the platform to get a ride up to the upper area. At the top, use the key to open a chest so that you can upgrade your tool with the blue star. Jump on up to the next higher area.

Pick up the plug inside and place it on one of the lava geysers.

STOP THE VOLCANO

A small volcano sits in the center of this area. Every so often, it erupts and sends out a scorching shock wave. Jump over the shock wave or you'll take a lot of damage.

Throw a water balloon on a seed in the back-left corner and use the tree that grows to get two more plugs from high platforms. Place those plugs on the other two geysers to stop the volcano from erupting.

EXIT THE LEVEL

After the geysers are plugged, a Brute appears to attack. Defeat him or just run for the exit to continue on to the final *Lion King* level.

Pick up a bomb and throw it at the target rocks on the right side.

Level 3

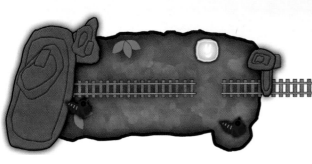

- Collectibles: 3 grubs
- Guests to Rescue: 2

LEGEND

Grub		Key
Challenge		VIC cube
Treasure chest		

BUILD THE TRACK

This level is like a shooting gallery. You board the Simba train and shoot at targets as you to. However, before you can get started, you must first repair the track. Find the missing section of track and move it into position.

DEFEAT THE ENEMIES

Now you have to face a Roto and its Fodder friends. Grab a VIC cube at the rear of the area and use the power-up for the fight.

GRUB

Pick up a water balloon and throw it at the seed on the front-left corner. Then jump up onto the tree to get a grub. Do the same in the front-right corner so you can also get the second grub. Be sure to get these before leaving this area. There is no coming back.

BOARD THE TRAIN

Now hop aboard the Simba train and take control of a cannon.

SHOOT THE RED TARGETS

As the train heads up to the top of Pride Rock, fire at the red targets to score points. Avoid hitting the blue targets that represent friendly animals.

When the train comes to a halt, shoot the spinner target to move the track into position so the train can continue. As you go through three shooting gallery areas, there is no minimum amount of targets you must hit. This is just a competition between players for the highest score.

> Some targets are worth more points than others because they are more difficult to hit. Try for the vultures since they are worth the most points.

DEFEAT SCAR

The Simba train eventually rolls into the final area where you must face off against Scar. Scar has two cannons— one on each shoulder. Use your cannon to attack him.

Before Scar fires one of his cannons, a target appears over that shoulder. Shoot the target quickly to prevent Scar from shooting at you. In the first stage, the target goes back and forth so as soon as you hit one, aim over the other shoulder so that you are ready to fire. Hitting the targets does not damage Scar. It only stops his attacks. So take a few shots at his head or body as you are moving between the targets.

After a few attacks, Scar rears back, exposing a target on his belly. Shoot it to prevent a slam attack and then take some shots at Scar's body.

When you have reduced Scar's health to nothing, as shown on the meter at the bottom of the screen, Scar collapses. However, he is not done yet.

Scar comes back for another round. This time he uses a cannon in his mouth. Two targets appear at the same time. Hit one to stop the first type of attack, then the other target to stop a second attack. As soon as you hit both targets, fire at the head and body.

Again Scar rears back and prepares for a slam attack. Shoot the target on his belly to stop the attack.

Keeping firing until you defeat Scar—for good this time—and he falls back, off the cliff.

FREE THE GUEST

GRUB

Move the drum on the left side of the area to the back and place it under the grub. Then jump onto the drum and shoot yourself up to get the third grub and unlock character models.

Challenge

After you defeat Scar, an arcade game appears. After all the competition in this level, why not play a challenge to wrap things up.

IT MEANS NO WORRIES!
By completing this level, and the entire *Lion King* world, you have earned this reward.

Move the drum to the right side and use it to get a key up on a ledge. Then carry the key to the back of the area to open a chest for a tool-upgrading blue star.

Finally, walk over and free the guest. As a reward, you unlock the Simba costume.

MONSTERS, INC. WALKTHROUGH

MONSTER TRAINING
Level 1

LEGEND

 Fuzzy dice

 Challenge

 Treasure chest

 Key

 VIC cube

 Exit

- Collectibles: 3 fuzzy dice
- Guests to Rescue: 0

GET INTO THE HOUSE

Monstropolis is a unique world where monsters live. Their society is powered by the screams of human children. What better place to learn about being a monster than at their training facility?

At the start, move to the right to find a key. Then carry it back to the chest on the left side of the area to quickly upgrade your tool with the blue star inside.

Next, step on all four red switches before the timer runs out. After you do this, the facade of the house drops and a door appears. Go through the door to enter the house.

GRAB THE KEYCARD

The house consists of several different rooms. In each, you must accomplish various objectives. In the first room, pull the lever on the right to make a platform rise, allowing you to jump up and get the keycard. Several enemies also appear. Defeat them and then pick up the keycard and take it over to the keycard reader. When a door appears, go through it to another room.

> Try pulling the lever on the left. It makes coins drop down from the ceiling.

FUZZY DICE

Step on the red switch and a platform lowers. Jump up onto it to get the fuzzy dice.

FIND THE KEYCARD

This room starts off with a fight as soon as you get in there. Defeat the Fodder, then pull on the lever at the back of the room. Step on the switches on the sides of the room to lower platforms. Jump up on them and move the cages down to the floor. Now pull the lever at the back to make a cage with a keycard in it rise up. Quickly move to the front of the room and pull the lever on the right. A laser moves across the room and cuts open all the cages. Be sure to jump over the laser and then take the keycard to the reader to bring in another door. Go through it to get to the next room.

WHERE IS THE KEYCARD?

Pull the lever at the back of the room and gravity is reversed—you are now walking on the ceiling. Since several enemies also appear, you have to fight upside down. After the enemies are gone, step on all the red switches on the ceiling and the pick up the keycard when it appears. Then pull the lever on the ceiling to drop to the floor. Pull the lever at the front of the room to raise a reader from the floor and then quickly take the keycard to the reader before time runs out. Head through the door to the next room.

> **Use the bombs in the room to blow open the cage with the coins—or to blow up other players.**

DEFEAT THE ENEMIES

Pull the lever in this room; the keycard appears in a large tube. A lot of Fodder also appear and attack. Fight off the enemies while you wait for the tube to lower so you can get the keycard.

USE THE KEYCARD

A Roto shows up when the Fodder are all toast. This is one tough enemy in a small room like this. Stay out of its way. Don't try to fight; just grab the keycard and take it to the reader, and then go through the doorway.

REVEAL THE KEYCARD

This room also has a fight right after you enter. Luckily it also has a VIC cube, so get a power-up and let 'em have it. Once you have won, pull the left-rear lever to raise up the keycard in a cage. Quickly pull the right-front lever to activate two laser beams. Jump over the low beam and stay down while the high beam passed by. Now pull the left-front lever to reverse gravity. More enemies arrive to fight. Defeat them and then pull the left lever on the ceiling to raise—or lower—a reader. Take the keycard to it before the timer runs out. Then go through the door that also appears on the ceiling.

SCARE THE CHILD

FUZZY DICE

Step on the red switch to lower a platform. Then jump up onto the platform to get the second pair of fuzzy dice.

Pull the lever to make a fake monster scare a child and produce scream. A tank of scream falls to the floor. Pick it up and take it through the door.

POWER UP THE EXIT

You are now outside the house and must take the scream canister to the power supply. However, you are not alone. Enemies arrive to try to stop you. Drop the canister and fight. Then, when it is clear, put the canister in the power supply.

EXIT THE LEVEL

FUZZY DICE

Before going through the exit, walk to the left to find a door. Go through it into a room in the house. Pull the lever at the back of the room to reverse gravity so you can get the fuzzy dice on the ceiling and unlock music. Pull the lever on the ceiling to drop down to the floor and go through the door to leave the house.

Challenge

When you come out of the house, an arcade game appears at the left side of the area. Use it to play a challenge and get some coins.

Go through the exit to get to the next level.

DISNEP TRIVIA

The Pizza Planet truck appears in all of the Disney.Pixar features and has become a tradition. In *Monsters, Inc.*, the truck is parked outside a trailer where Randall is sent near the end of the movie.

Level 2

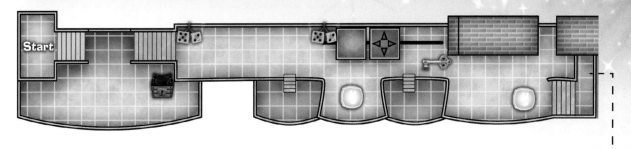

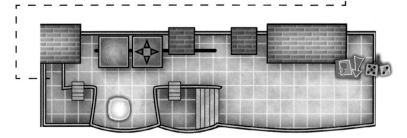

LEGEND

🎲	Fuzzy dice	🔑	Key
👹	Challenge	⬜	VIC cube
📦	Treasure chest	📄	Exit

- Collectibles: 3 fuzzy dice
- Guests to Rescue: 0

CROSS THE BARRIER

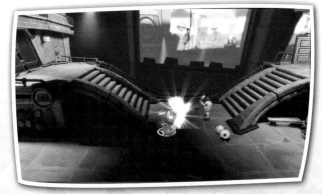

The enemies here like to fight. They attack right at the beginning of the level. Defeat them all and then continue moving to the right.

FUZZY DICE

Walk up the stairs to the right and stand by the door. Wait until the door at the top moves next to the fuzzy dice, then go through the door to get the dice.

Wait until the door moves to the right past the barrier, then walk through the door again to get past the barrier. Step on the red switch to lower the barrier. Continue to the right and fight off an attack and clear this area.

Keep going to the right to find a key. Then take it back to the chest near the start to get a blue star that upgrades your tool.

Now jump up onto the mobile lift and pull the lever to lower the lift.

FUZZY DICE

Step on the left arrow to make the lift go to the left. When you are as far as you can go, step on the back arrow to raise the lift. Jump off to the left to get the pair of fuzzy dice.

Pull on the lever to lower the lift again, then move it to the right, past the barrier. Then raise it up so you can get to the door. Go through into the room.

SCARE THE CHILD

Inside the room, pull on the lever to scare the child. Pick up the canister and carry it through the door. Drop down to the floor and fight against lots of enemies.

Carry the canister down the stairs and insert it into a power supply. You need one more canister. Go through the door on the main floor to enter a room and scare anther child. Bring that canister down to the power supply to extend a bridge to the right. Walk across to the next area.

You have another fight to win against the enemies. Use the VIC cube in this area, then continue to the right when you've defeated the enemies.

BUILD THE DOOR

To use the broken doorway, you must find the three pieces of the door and bring them to the door frame. The first is near the frame, so pick it up and carry it to the frame.

As soon as you pick up the first piece of the door, a new enemy appears—the Bulldog. Several Fodder join it in attacking you. Avoid its charges and keep moving, getting in slam attacks on the beast when you can.

Bulldog

The Bulldog is a mini-boss that is typically assigned to guard a location—one that players need to get to. Bulldogs charge any players who get close to their area. As you are being charged, watch for a button icon to appear. Quickly press that button to avoid the charge and put yourself in a position to counterattack the Bulldog. The key to defeating a Bulldog is to avoid its charges and after it is recovering from a charge, move in to hit it with slam attacks.

BAD DOG!
Defeat your first Bulldog to earn this award.

Put the first piece of the door in the frame and then head to the left. You need the mobile lift to get the second piece. Drive it to the right and raise the lift. Jump onto a wooden platform and then on to the roof of a room to get the piece. Pick it up and carry it to the frame.

Move to the right and use the door near the exit to get into an upper balcony overlooking the training area. Pick up the last door piece and take it back to the frame.

FUZZY DICE

While you are getting the final door piece in the upper balcony, be sure to collect the third pair of fuzzy dice and unlock some concept art.

POWER THE EXIT

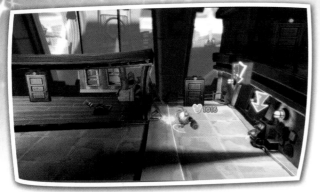

Now that the door is completed, move through it to enter the practice room. Pull the lever to scare the child and then carry the canister to the power supply by the exit.

EXIT THE LEVEL

Move through the blue exit to get to the last level of the Monster Training location.

Level 3

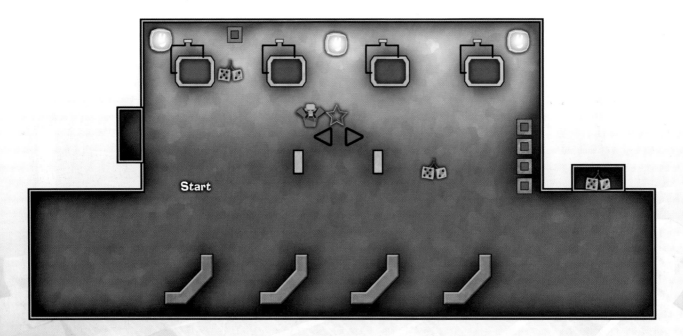

Start

LEGEND

Fuzzy dice

Challenge

VIC cube

Star

- Collectibles: 3 fuzzy dice
- Guests to Rescue: 2

START THE DOOR SYSTEM

This level is contained within one large room. Start off by moving to the center and picking up the keycard. Carry it to the reader to get things going.

COLLECT THE SCREAM CANISTERS

FUZZY DICE

Step on the four red switches on the right side of the level to open a door. Inside is the first pair of fuzzy dice.

After using the keycard, four pairs of doors are brought in. There are canisters next to two of the top doors. The doors are color-coded so that you'll know where you end up when you go through one. Move through the yellow door on the bottom to get to the yellow door on top.

Pick up the canister and then drop down from the platform and carry it to the canister slot. Go get the second canister by walking through the white door; bring the canister to the other slot.

When both canisters are in the slots, the doors are carried away and enemies appear to attack. Defeat them to make more doors arrive.

Pull on the lever between the canister slots to make electrical charges zap anyone next to the slots. This works great against enemies—as well as other players. Enemies like to use this, too, so be careful when fighting near the canister slots.

Collect two more canisters from the new set of doors and carry them to the slots. Then be ready for another wave of enemies to attack.

FUZZY DICE

After the second set of doors leaves and enemies arrive, a pair of fuzzy dice is dropped off in the back-left area of the floor. Go pick them up and add them to your collection.

The third set of doors is a bit different. The colors of the bottom doors change. So look at the doors on top with a canister next to them, then wait for the door you are standing near to change to that color. Get both canisters back to the slots.

Press the red switch at the back of the room to open a door on the left side where a large coin is waiting for you.

FUZZY DICE

After completing the third set of doors, the third pair of fuzzy dice appears to the right of the canister slots. Pick them up and unlock character models.

Defeat another wave of enemies and then get to work on the fourth set of doors. This time the top doors move back and forth. Stay at a bottom door and when the top door of the same color is next to a canister, move through it. Bring both canisters to the slots.

Now you must face a Roto and some other enemies. Plus, a long tube drops off a blue star in the middle. Go after the blue star to upgrade your tool. The star is only there for a short time before another tube drops down and sucks it up—never to be seen again.

This area is great for fighting the Roto—plenty of space to move around, as well as bombs to throw at it.

There are only two more canisters to go. This time, you can move the top doors by pressing on the arrow switches near the lever. Bring both canisters to the slots.

Challenge

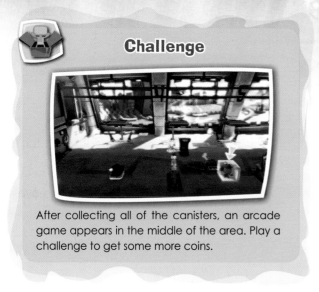

After collecting all of the canisters, an arcade game appears in the middle of the area. Play a challenge to get some more coins.

FREE THE GUEST

To finish this level and location, free the guest. You also unlock the Timon costume.

Complete Monster Training again to rescue another guest and unlock the BURN-E costume.

HIGH IN THE HIMALAYAS

Level 1

LEGEND

Fuzzy dice		Key	
Challenge		VIC cube	
Treasure chest		Exit	

- Collectibles: 3 fuzzy dice
- Guests to Rescue: 0

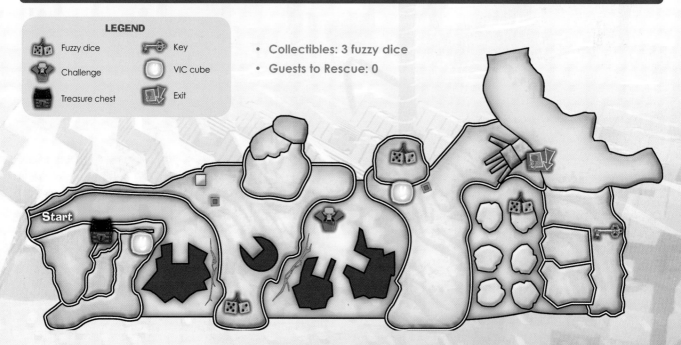

Start

WAKE THE MONSTER

You are not longer in Monstropolis. Instead, you are in the snowy Himalayan mountains. Start off by picking up the nearby lantern. This item melts right through ice and saves a lot of hits with your tool. You can find a lot of coins hidden in ice cubes and small ice mounds.

Slide down the icy slope and pick up the VIC cube so that you are ready for the first enemy attack.

Watch out for the cracks with icy vapors coming out. If the vapor touches you, a block of ice covers you. Press the Use button repeatedly to break free. Pick up and throw enemies—or even other players—at these cracks to freeze them and get them out of the picture for a while.

FUZZY DICE

With a lantern in hand, walk toward the front of the area and melt the ice surrounding the first pair of fuzzy dice.

Continue all the way to the right. Use the lantern, or slam attacks, to free the ice from the crank. Then turn the crank to open the cave door. The monster wakes up and throws three snow cones out into the icy cold.

RETRIEVE THE SNOW CONES

The first snow cone is just to the left. Go pick it up and then take it back and place it into the monster's giant hand.

FUZZY DICE

Go back to where you picked up the first snow cone, then move to the right and jump out onto the ice flows in a river. Collect another pair of fuzzy dice floating in the air above the middle of the river.

Continue across the icy river to find the second snow cone. Take it back to the monster.

The second door piece is located in the left part of the level in a low area created when the ice cracks. Pick it up and carry it back to the frame.

The key is near the snow cone on the right side of the river. Pick it up and take it back to the chest, which is near where you began the level. Get a blue star to upgrade your tool.

Step on fan switches and giant fans appear and blow a strong wind. Use these to blow both enemies and other players out of your way.

The last snow cone is up on a ledge. However, you need to fix a door to get to it. Use the lantern to melt the stack of ice blocks at the back of the area and use the stone blocks as steps to get to the door piece. Carry it to the frame to the left. You have to fight enemies as you do this.

The last piece of door is located in another low area to the right of the frame. Get it to the door to complete the repair.

Challenge

FUZZY DICE

After jumping up the stone blocks to get the first door piece, pick up a third pair of fuzzy dice while you are there and unlock some music.

As soon as the door is fixed, an arcade game appears just to the right. Stop by and play a challenge.

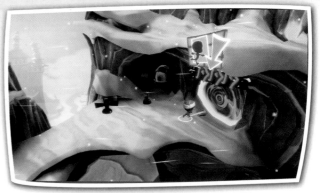

EXIT THE LEVEL

Go through the door to get the last snow cone. Take it back to the monster to open the exit.

A Roto and more enemies appear as you fix the door. You can fight them if you want or just take the snow cone to the monster as quickly as you can.

Once you are ready to leave this level and continue on to the next, move through the exit.

Disney TRIVIA

Posters of Disneyland attractions appear in Boo's bedroom as well as the Monstropolis travel office.

Level 2

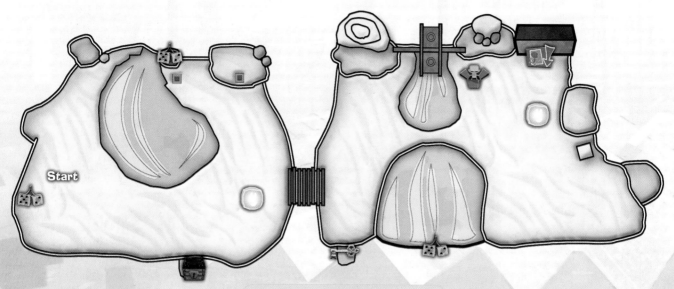

Start

LEGEND

	Fuzzy dice		Key
	Challenge		VIC cube
	Treasure chest		Exit

- Collectibles: 3 fuzzy dice
- Guests to Rescue: 0

USE THE SNOWMOBILE

You are still in the snow, but now have some extra firepower—the snowmobile, which is essentially a cannon on skis. However, before going to the snowmobile, grab a lantern and melt some ice to get coins.

FUZZY DICE

The first pair of fuzzy dice is just to the left of the entrance. Carefully melt the ice blocks, leaving one on the right side so that you can use the ice block and stone blocks to jump up and get the dice.

As you advance to the right toward the snowmobile, enemies attack. Fight them off so they won't bother you while you get your work done.

FUZZY DICE

There are more fuzzy dice by the snowmobile. Carefully use the lantern to melt some of the ice blocks. Leave three on the left side. Jump up the blocks to get the dice. You can also step on the red switch on the ledge to the right to open a door to get a big coin.

Before using the snowmobile, follow a pathway down to the right at the front of the area. You pass by a cave with a chest inside. Carefully move along an icy, slippery path to the right. Jump across a gap and then continue to the end to find the key. Take it back to the chest to get a blue star and upgrade your tool.

> When playing with other players, grab a lantern and take off, melting ice to get as many coins as you can. Let the others deal with the enemies. They may be so focused on the fight, they don't even notice you taking all the loot.

RAISE THE BRIDGE

Return to the snowmobile and hop aboard. Drive it to the right and use it to shoot the large target to raise the bridge so that you can cross.

BUILD THE BROKEN DOOR

Drive the snowmobile across the bridge toward the targets on the wheel. However, before shooting, get off the snowmobile and fight the enemies in the area. Be sure to stop the Fodder from building a cannon trap near the exit or it can cause trouble.

Once the area is clear, climb back onto the snowmobile and fire at the targets to turn the wheel and open a door to the right. Then pick up the door piece and carry it to the frame on the left.

Fight off more enemies that appear after you place the piece in the door. Then drive the snowmobile to the front-right corner of the level. Blast through an ice wall to find the second door piece. Carry it back to the frame.

Challenge

After you place the second piece in the door frame, an arcade game appears by the target wheel. Take a moment to play a challenge.

While you are going after the third door piece, more enemies, including a mini-boss, arrive to attack. It is easiest to defeat them all first, then continue working on your current objective.

The last door piece is over by the bridge and surrounded by ice. Either use the lantern to melt the ice or perform slam attacks to break it. Take the door piece back to the frame to complete this task.

POWER UP THE EXIT

After going through the door, pick up the canister on top of the ledge and carry it over to the power supply by the exit. You may have to stop and fight several enemies along the way. Place the canister into the power supply.

EXIT THE LEVEL

Finally, move through the exit to get to the next level.

Level 3

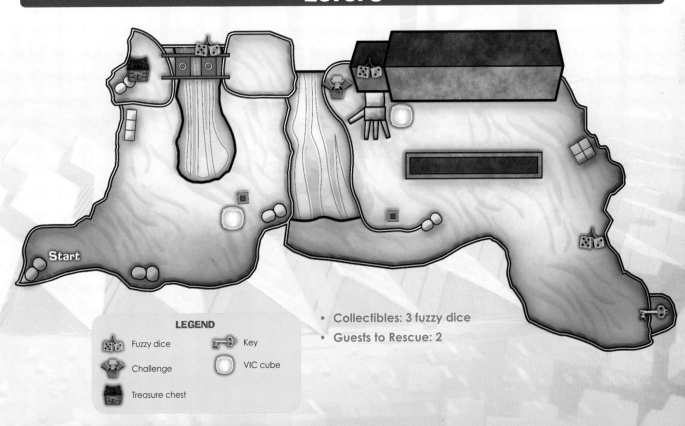

Start

LEGEND

Fuzzy dice   Key

Challenge   VIC cube

Treasure chest

- Collectibles: 3 fuzzy dice
- Guests to Rescue: 2

WAKE THE MONSTER

This level begins with a fight as you move away from the starting area. Deal with the enemies and try to prevent them from constructing traps.

Move the crank over to its slot and then take some time to explore the area before turning the crank.

Head down from the fuzzy dice to find a key. Carry it all the way back toward a wall of ice and stone blocks on the level's left side. Melt all of the ice blocks with a lantern, then carry the key to the ledge on top and open a chest for a blue star that upgrades your tool.

FUZZY DICE

Move all the way to the far-right side of the level and get rid of the ice surrounding the first pair of fuzzy dice so you can pick them up.

Now go ahead and turn the crank to wake the monster. Once again, he throws three snow cones out into the cold.

RETRIEVE THE SNOW CONES

Fight off the enemies that appear, then hop onto the snowmobile. Fire at the targets to make a bridge so that you can get to the snow cone up on the ledge above the monster's giant eye.

FUZZY DICE

The second pair of fuzzy dice is hiding behind the targets. After shooting the targets to make the bridge, walk to the edge of the frozen river and jump up to get the dice.

The next snow cone is moved around by enemies, so it can be tough to find. It is usually near the front of the level on the left side. Once you locate it, carry it back to the hand.

Climb up the blocks and jump across the bridge to get to the first snow cone. Pick it up and drop down to the ground below. Take it to the monster's giant hand.

Challenge

As soon as you make it across the bridge, an arcade machine appears below. Be sure to use it to play a challenge before you leave this level.

A mini-boss and Fodder appear right after you deliver the second snow cone. Take the time to defeat them and use a VIC cube to help you with a power-up.

Melt or break the ice blocks along the far-right side of the level. Jump up the stone blocks to get the third snow cone.

FUZZY DICE

While on the ledge with the snow cone, jump across to the right and land in the damaged roof of the nearby shack to get the third pair of fuzzy dice. Doing so unlocks character models.

RAISE THE SNOWBALL TURRETS

The monster gives you a scream canister in exchange for the snow cones. Pick it up and carry it to the power supply to raise a snowball turret for each player.

USE THE SNOWBALL TURRETS TO SHOOT ENEMIES

Take control of a turret and start shooting at enemies as they open the windows. You need to score 20 points to complete this shooting game. Brutes are worth 3 points and Fodder only one point each. However, you have to hit the Brutes more than once to knock them down.

Watch out for some of these enemies. If they stay in the window too long, they throw snowballs at you that knock you off the turret and turn you into a block of ice.

If you hit the target gong, Fodder run out of the building and attack. You must get off the cannon and defeat them before continuing.

When you hit a skull target, all turrets are disabled for a short amount of time. Keep shooting until someone gets 20 points.

FREE THE GUEST

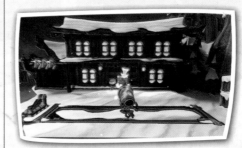

Now go up and free the guest. You unlock the Stitch costume as a reward.

Play this level again to free another guest and unlock the Ariel costume.

DOOR FACTORY

Level 1

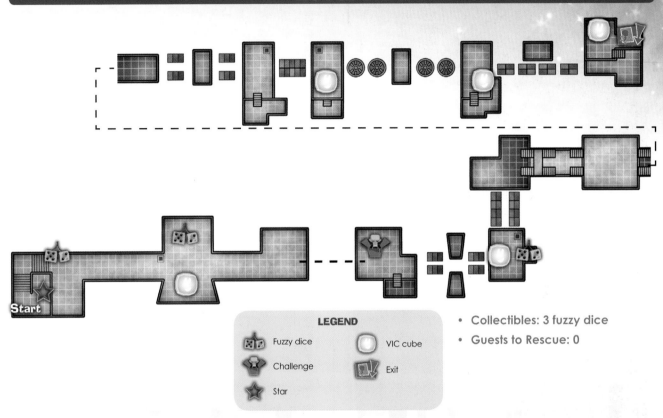

LEGEND

Fuzzy dice		VIC cube	
Challenge		Exit	
Star			

- Collectibles: 3 fuzzy dice
- Guests to Rescue: 0

EXPLORE THE FACTORY

You begin on the left side of the level. First, look at the colored symbols on the door to the right. Then duplicate that pattern on the controls using the footprint pads. Once you have the same pattern, the door opens and you can get a blue star to upgrade your tool. Fight off any enemies that come after you, then head up the stairs.

NAVIGATE PAST THE DOORS

FUZZY DICE

At the top of the stairs, go through the door next to the wall. This takes you up onto a narrow walkway. Go to the end to get a pair of fuzzy dice. Then go back through the door to get to the main area.

You now have to get past lots of moving doors. Watch the traffic-style light on the wall. When it is red, doors are moving across the floor. Wait until they pass and the light turns green before quickly moving across to the other side of the rails.

You face a lot of enemies throughout the factory. Whenever you see enemies appearing, look around. I have placed VIC cubes in many places to help you defeat the enemies. The power-ups can come in handy.

FUZZY DICE

Step on the red switch to halt the doors here so that you can walk out onto a platform and get a second pair of fuzzy dice. Once you have them, head back to the walkway and continue past a door crossing.

Fight some enemies and then watch the doors to the right. They come up, pause, flip over, pause, and then go down. As soon as they stop, jump across to the set near the back of the area and then jump to the platform and pick up the keycard.

GRAB THE DOORS

Jump across some more doors to get to a larger platform. Fight the Brute and other enemies to clear the platform so that you can use the keycard.

Stand on the pad by the edge of the platform and press the Use button as the door moves over you. Keep holding onto the button as the door takes you across a gap and then release the button to drop down onto the platform on the other side.

FUZZY DICE

Place the keycard in the reader to open the door. Pick up the third pair of fuzzy dice and unlock music.

Challenge

As soon as you drop from the door, an arcade machine appears. Take some time to play a challenge.

CROSS THE GAP

Step on the red switch to slow down the two rows of moving doors. Jump across on them to get to the platform on the other side.

DODGE THE DOORS

Fight another wave of enemies. Then get ready to move past some doors. These doors are coming straight at you. While you are in the low areas, they can't hit you. However, when you go up the steps to the higher areas, you can get hit. Watch the lights. When they are green, go. Stop in the middle low area since the second high area is wider and takes longer to cross.

Jump across two more sets of flipping doors to get to another platform, where you have to battle against more enemies.

The next obstacles are doors that flip up and down. Press the red switch to drop all of the doors down and then begin the cycle over. As soon as the doors in front of you come up, start moving across. Don't stop since they drop right behind you. Hurry to the end.

When playing with other players, wait until they start moving across and then step on the red switch. Or if you get to the end first, step on the red switch on that side. Either way, your opponents will fall and this give you a chance to gather all the coins on the platform.

Now you have to jump across to two rotating turbines. Doors move between the turbines, so watch for the green light. Since they are turning, be careful when you jump; the motion of the turbine can throw off your aim a bit. After getting to a small platform, go across two more turbines.

The next part is not too tough. Four sets of doors are arranged like paddles. Jump onto the left side, ride it to the right, and then jump over to the next set. Keep going until you get to the platform.

Next, turn the crank to increase pressure in the pipe until it bursts and a canister falls out. Once both canisters are in the power supply, the door opens.

POWER THE DOOR

EXIT THE LEVEL

Finally, move through the exit to get to the next level.

You now have to get two scream canisters to supply power to open the door. First defeat all the enemies and then step on all four red switches before the timer runs out to get the first canister. Carry it over to the power supply by the door.

DISNEY TRIVIA

In Boo's room in the movie, there is a Nemo toy, a Jessie doll, and a Pixar ball.

Level 2

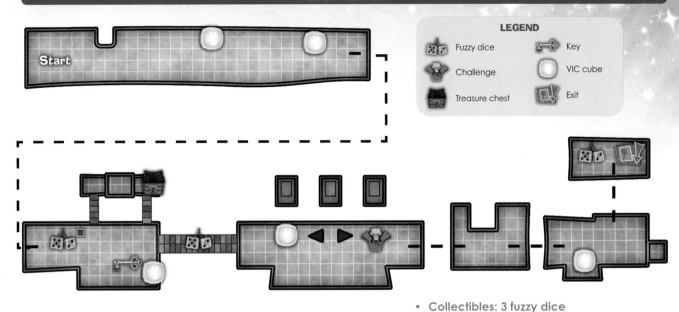

- Collectibles: 3 fuzzy dice
- Guests to Rescue: 0

EXPLORE THE FACTORY

Start this level by moving to the right and fighting a bunch of enemies. Clear them out.

Go through the door and emerge from a door on the ceiling—upside down. Move to the sides at the front of the area when the light turns red and doors move past. Then advance to the right, collecting coins as you go. Go through the door at the right side to emerge back on the ground.

DESTROY THE DOORS

Ahead of you a series of doors blocks your way. Pick up bombs and throw them at the doors to blast a way through so you can get to the other side.

FUZZY DICE

Blow up every single door so that none remain. A pair of fuzzy dice appears for you to collect.

After fighting some enemies, press the red switch here and quickly move across a bridge of doors. Press another red switch to make more doors rise up to form a bridge. Come back across and pull the green lever to stop the doors moving across the middle of the platform. Move quickly because the bridges are on a timer.

When you get to the platform, quickly grab a key in the front-right corner. Then quickly move to the first red switch on the left and get across the door bridge to the chest on the far platform. The blue star inside upgrades your tool.

FUZZY DICE

Press the red switch on the right side to slow down the conveyor belt of doors for a short time. Quickly move across the doors, picking up a second pair of fuzzy dice along the way.

POWER UP THE DOORS

You now need to get two scream canisters. After fighting a wave of enemies, move to the arrow switches.

Use them to move the far door to the left or right so it is positioned over one of the three incinerators. Watch the lights on the incinerators. When all three are red, the trap door opens and flames shoot up. As soon as the incinerator you are going to has three green lights, quickly go through the door. Pick up the canister and wait until the trap door opens. When it closes, move through the door to get back to the platform and carry the canister to the power supply.

Challenge

As soon as you put the second canister into the power supply, an arcade game appears near the arrow switches. Use it to play a challenge.

CROSS THE GAP

Now that the doors are moving, stand on the pad and hold down the Use button as a door passes over you. Ride it across to another platform, where you must fight against a lot of enemies. Then jump over to another, larger platform.

DESTROY THE DOORS

Here you must fight against a Brute and other enemies. Be sure to use the VIC cube and bombs to help you win this battle.

> There is a door on the right side of this area. Enter the code found above the door into the console to the side of the door to open it and get a big coin.

Now move over by the pile of bombs and throw them at the red doors. You need to destroy only a few to create a way to get to the exit.

FUZZY DICE

Blow up all of the red doors by the exit to make a third pair of fuzzy dice appear. Pick them up to unlock concept art.

EXIT THE LEVEL

Go through the door to get to the other platform. Then continue into the exit to start the next level.

Disney TRIVIA

Pixar likes to have some common things in all its movies. Like the Pizza Planet truck, they also have a voice actor appear in all Pixar features. John Ratzenberger is in all of the movies and voices the Abominable Snowman in *Monsters, Inc.*

Level 3

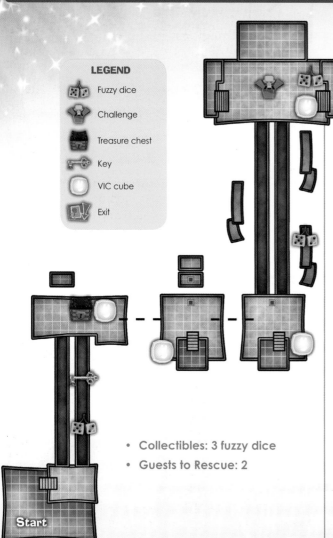

LEGEND

- Fuzzy dice
- Challenge
- Treasure chest
- Key
- VIC cube
- Exit

- Collectibles: 3 fuzzy dice
- Guests to Rescue: 2

Start

GET READY

Stand in the glowing light.

Step onto the footprint pad. A timer begins to countdown. You have to race along a conveyor belt. Jump to the other belt when doors come at you. Choppers are following close behind you, so you have to keep moving.

FUZZY DICE

Jump across to the right conveyor belt to get the pair of fuzzy dice. Then go back to the left to avoid doors.

There is a key on the right side as well. Pick it up as you run past it. Avoid getting hit as you take it to the chest on the platform ahead to get a blue star for upgrading your tool.

OPEN THE GATES

At the start, move to the left and pick up the keycard. Take it to the reader by the gates.

POWER THE DOORS

You need to get two scream canisters for power. The first is lying on the platform. Defeat all of the enemies, then carry it over to the power supply on the right side.

The other canister is on a platform surrounded by moving doors. Use bombs to blow up enough doors so that you can move in to get the canister and then take it to the power supply.

Move over to the pad and, as a door passes over you, hold down the Use button. Ride it across to another platform and then release the button to drop down.

USE THE SCREAM CANISTERS

After fighting off more enemies, step on the red switch to move a platform toward you. Jump over to it and then ride it to a far platform with a canister. Pick it up and jump over to the moving platform. Stand on the red switch to make it move toward you again. Jump across to the main platform and put the canister in the power supply.

Move down to a lower area and turn a crank to build up pressure in a pipe. A canister falls out when the pipe bursts. Pick it up and carry it to the power supply. Jump on the pad to get up to the higher area. Then grab onto a door and ride it over to the next platform.

OPEN THE GATES

You must fight more enemies on this platform. A VIC cube is in the front-right corner, so get it for a power-up.

Then pick up the keycard in the lower area and place it in the reader to open the gates and start another conveyor belt race.

FUZZY DICE

As you are racing, jump over to the right conveyor belt. Then, as the doors are coming at you, jump over to a platform on the right to get the fuzzy dice. Jump back onto the belt and finish the race.

LOWER THE DOORS

Move to the left side of this large platform and turn the crank to lower a row of doors into position.

DEFEAT THE FAULTY DOORS

FUZZY DICE

Jump on the pad on the right side to bounce up to get the third pair of fuzzy dice and unlock character models.

The faulty door moves across the platform firing a laser beam. Jump over it as it passes by one way and then comes back again.

When it stops, move a door claw to a position underneath it using the arrow switches. Then step on the square switch to grab onto the door and send it to the chopper.

Now you have to fight against a wave of enemies that includes a mini-boss.

Turn the crank clockwise again to bring another faulty door down. This door fires blobs at you. Dodge them and then, when it stops, use the claw to grab the door and get rid of it.

134

Fight off some more enemies and turn the crank again. The third faulty door launches fireballs at you. Stay out of their way and then destroy this door as well.

More enemies attack, including a mini-boss. As before, beat them all so that you can turn the crank. The fourth door fires three energy beams. Jump over them and, when the door stops, grab it with the claw and chop it up.

Fight off a final wave of enemies and then turn the crank to lower a platform with the guest on it down to your level.

FREE THE GUEST

Challenge

As you turn the crank, an arcade game appears in the middle of the area. Walk over and use it to play a challenge for some coins.

Now walk over to the guest and set it free. In return for your efforts, the Mike costume is unlocked.

Play the Door Factory levels again to rescue another guest and unlock the Sully costume.

SCARY FEET!
Complete the *Monsters, Inc.* world to earn this award.

ALADDIN WALKTHROUGH

CAVE OF WONDERS

Level 1

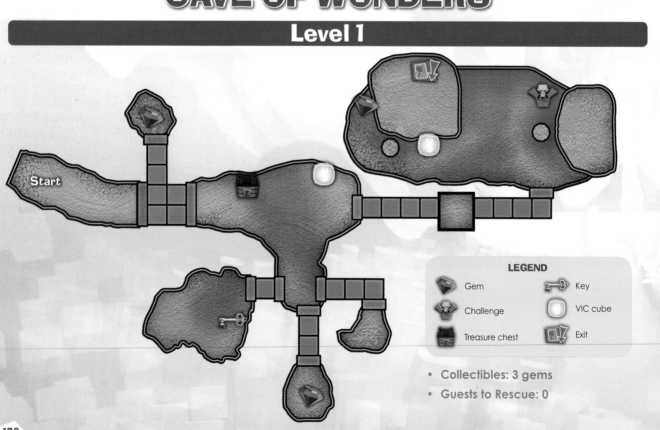

Start

LEGEND

💎	Gem	🔑	Key	
🏺	Challenge	🔲	VIC cube	
📦	Treasure chest	📇	Exit	

- Collectibles: 3 gems
- Guests to Rescue: 0

BUILD THE SCARAB

FIND THE SCARAB PIECES

The first location in the *Aladdin* world is the Cave of Wonders. The magic is strong in this level and things can appear and disappear right in front of your eyes.

Another scarab is flying toward the front of the area. Wait for it to fly to the left and reveal a bridge, or jump over the gap, to find another scarab piece along with a key. When the flying scarab returns, move the scarab piece across the small bridge and take it to another statue. Then take the key to the chest by the statue to get a blue star for upgrading your tool.

From the start, walk over to the scarab piece on the ground and move it over to the statue to assemble a scarab.

As the scarab flies over the gap to the right, sections of a bridge appear. Move across quickly since the sections disappear as the scarab flies away.

Now pick up another scarab piece located to the right of the previous piece and take it back to the statue to release another flying scarab. Then follow this scarab up a series of bridge sections to the right to find the lantern.

UNCOVER SECRETS IN THE SAND

BUILD THE SCARAB

The lantern is a very useful tool. As you move it around, it illuminates bridge sections and allows you to move across them without a scarab flying over. It also reveals things hidden in the sand.

Place the lantern over the sparkling sand near the bombs to reveal another scarab piece. Move it to the statue.

GEM

Move the lantern down the platform and toward the place where you entered the Cave of Wonders. The lantern causes bridge sections to appear so you can move across to the first gem.

GEM

Take the lantern to the front of the area between the two platforms where you found the scarab pieces. There you can find the second gem.

Now move the lantern to the right to make a short pillar appear. Jump up on this to get onto the ledge on the right and move another scarab piece to the statute. A flying scarab then moves to open the exit.

Challenge

Now move the lantern all the way to the right and up the bridge sections to the upper area of this level. There, you must defeat more enemies, including a Roto. Pick up the VIC cube to the left and use the power-up for the fight.

As soon as you build the scarab on the upper area, an arcade game appears. Play a challenge to get more coins.

EXIT THE LEVEL

GEM

Move the lantern to the far-left side of the upper area to reveal the third gem. Collect it to unlock some music.

Finally, use the lantern to reveal a short pillar at the edge of the left ledge so that you can get up to the exit. Go through it to continue to the next level.

Disney TRIVIA

The movie *Aladdin* was so popular that Disney produced two sequels—*Aladdin: The Return of Jafar* and *Aladdin and the King of Thieves*—as well as an animated television series.

Level 2

LEGEND

Gem		Key	
Challenge		VIC cube	
Treasure chest		Exit	

- Collectibles: 3 gems
- Guests to Rescue: 0

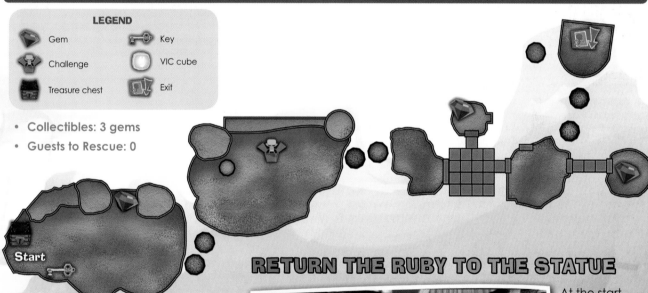

Start

RETURN THE RUBY TO THE STATUE

At the start, fight against some enemies as they try to stop you from getting the lantern. One may even try to carry it away.

Move the lantern around to reveal coins and a key. Use this key to open the nearby chest to get a blue star and upgrade your tool to the next level.

Take the lantern over by the monkey statue to reveal a small pillar. Jump up onto it and then onto the ledge to the left. Pick up the ruby and take it to the monkey statue.

A series of stone steps appear. Jump up them to get to the upper area.

RETURN THE RUBY TO THE STATUE

Defeat more enemies here so you can get the lantern away from them.

GEM

Take the lantern to the front of the upper area to reveal a red switch. Step on it to make the monkey statue below, where you already returned a ruby, rise up to reveal a gem. Jump back down the stone steps to get the gem. Then come back up to the upper area.

Try to get the lanterns before the other players. This lets you decide where you want to search and gives you first access to the gold. You can also use a lantern to get across bridge sections and leave the others behind for a bit.

Move the lantern over by the crank to raise a short pillar. Jump up to the crank and turn it. A gear along the back wall moves a ruby up and drops it onto a ramp.

Now take the lantern over by the monkey statue to reveal another red switch. Stand on the switch to lower a section of stone that is blocking the ruby. Once the stone is lowered, the ruby rolls into the monkey statue.

As some more stone steps appear to the right, a Bulldog begins attacking. Watch out for its charging and get in some hits as it pauses at the end of its attacks.

Challenge

Putting the ruby in the second monkey statue causes an arcade game to appear. Use it to play a challenge.

RETURN THE RUBY TO THE STATUE

Jump up the stone steps to get to another area. Use the lantern to move across some bridge sections to get to another area where a ruby is waiting for you.

GEM

Move the lantern farther to the right and across more bridge sections to find the second gem.

Position two lanterns on the bridge sections so that they stay visible. Then carry the last ruby to the monkey statue to open the exit.

GEM

Move a lantern to the area to the left of the monkey statue to find the third gem and unlock some concept art.

EXIT THE LEVEL

Finally, walk back to where you found the last ruby, fight off some enemies, and then jump across some stone steps to get to the exit. Go through and get ready for the next level.

Level 3

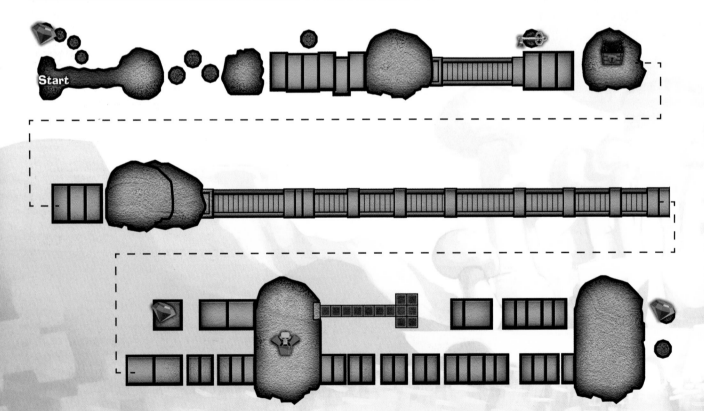

Start

LEGEND

Gem

Challenge

Treasure chest

Key

- Collectibles: 3 gems
- Guests to Rescue: 2

FIND THE LAMP

Collect some coins at the start and be sure to destroy the cobra statue.

Watch out for falling rocks and pillars as you go. Pick up what coins you can along the way, but don't lag behind.

GEM

Jump across a series of stone steps to get to the first gem. These steps collapse soon after you step on them, so be quick and accurate. You get only one chance to get this gem.

After dodging a rolling boulder as you climb some steps, jump across to a stone platform to grab a key. Quickly jump back before the platform collapses.

Walk up the ramp to the right to find the lamp. However, before you can get it, Jafar comes by on a magic carpet and steals it away from you.

ESCAPE THE CAVE

Take the key to the chest just a bit farther to the right and quickly open it to get a blue star for upgrading your tool.

Jump across some stone steps and then onto some platforms. Keep moving to the right. A giant wave of lava is following behind you. It is now a race to stay in front of the lava.

Watch out for more rolling boulders. Dodge them and keep moving up the steps to the top where you must grab a scarab piece and move it to the right.

GEM

Place the scarab piece in the statue to release a flying scarab. Jump over the trap and follow the scarab as it reveals bridge sections that lead to the second gem.

 As you come across spike traps, just jump over them. You don't have time to smash them.

Challenge

When you get to the place where the two paths converge, stop by the arcade machine to take a break from running and play a challenge.

A lantern is by the arcade game. Use it to reveal a path of bridge sections at the back of the level. This allows you to avoid spikes and pick up gold as you go.

As you come across a ruby along the front pathway, pick it up and carry it all the way to the end. Don't die or you drop the ruby.

GEM

Take the ruby to the monkey statue and place it in the statue's hands. Some stone steps appear to the right. Jump up them to get the third gem and unlock some character models.

FREE THE GUEST

Finally, free the guest being help prisoner and unlock the M-O costume.

Complete the Cave of Wonder a second time and save another guest to unlock the Gibbs costume.

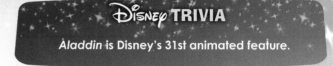

Disney TRIVIA

Aladdin is Disney's 31st animated feature.

STREETS OF AGRABAH
Level 1

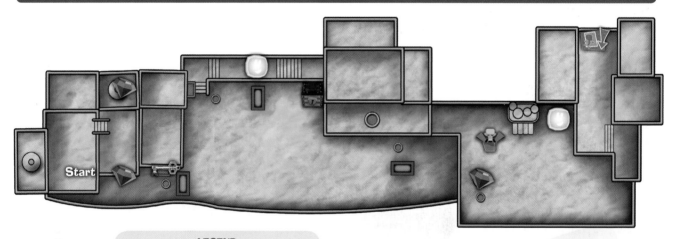

LEGEND

◆	Gem	🔑	Key
✦	Challenge	⬜	VIC cube
📦	Treasure chest	🗂	Exit

- Collectibles: 3 gems
- Guests to Rescue: 0

GET TO GROUND LEVEL

Agrabah is a city of mystery and enchant-ment—and the finest merchandise this side of the River Jordan. Here, you encounter some new things to help you open areas and you also use the lamp.

GEM

At the start, pick up a bomb and throw it at the dome to the right to find the first gem.

Make your way to the right across the rooftops and then drop down to the street below where all the action takes place.

GET THE LAMP

As soon as you get to the street, start fighting the enemies and stop them from building traps. Defeat them all, including a Roto that shows up just as you think the battle is over.

The street performers can help you get to places using their abilities. Drag the snake charmer with the flute and the green rug over to the green pad on the left side. As he plays, a rope rises up. Climb it to get the key. Take the key to the chest near where you found the snake charmer and upgrade your tool with a blue star.

There are four different types of street performers in Agrabah, although only two types appear in this level. Each functions only on a pad that is the same color as the performer's rug. So if you see those rectangular pads, start looking for a performer.

Now drag the snake charmer over to the green pad on the right. Climb up the rope and get the lamp.

USE THE LAMP TO TRANSFORM THINGS

Place the lamp on the round pad to open the curtain and move to the other part of this level. As soon as you use the lamp, enemies appear. Defeat them and then pick up the lamp. Continue through the building and to the area to the right.

COMPLETE THE ACROBATIC DISPLAY

Place the lamp on the round pad near the musical instrument stall. It transforms the stall into a giant pipe organ.

GEM

Go back to the first area near where the key was located. Look at the colors of the notes above a door. Go back to the organ and play those notes in the same order by jumping onto those keys. This opens the door so you can get the gem inside.

On your way back, get the acrobat in the first area and move him to the gray pad in the second area.

Several enemies, including a Brute, show up and attack. Use the VIC cube for a power-up to help defeat them.

There is another door to the right of the acrobats with notes above it. Play those notes on the giant organ to open this door. Then move the acrobat inside out to the gray pad to complete the display and open the exit.

Challenge

As soon as you move the second acrobat into position, an arcade game appears near the organ. Be sure to play a challenge before you leave this level.

EXIT THE LEVEL

GEM

Move the lamp to the round pad by the well to create a geyser that carries you up to get the third gem and unlock some music.

Finally, stand on the footprint pad by the acrobats and press the use button. The acrobats will get you up to the higher level; go through the exit and continue to the next level.

Level 2

Start

- Collectibles: 3 gems
- Guests to Rescue: 0

LEGEND

Gem		Star	
Challenge		Exit	
VIC cube			

BURN THE CAGES

You begin in a courtyard along with a fire-eating street performer. Move the fire-eater onto the red pads to burn the cages.

Stand on the footprint pad and press the Use button to pull on the handle and open the courtyard door. You can get into the streets.

GET THE LAMP

Pick up the VIC cube and start fighting against all the enemies attacking you or building traps. You need to clear the streets. Toward the end of the fight, a Bulldog appears, so be ready.

Jump on a small trampoline to get up onto a roof where the lamp is located. Pick it up and then jump back down to the street.

USE THE LAMP TO TRANSFORM THINGS

Place the lamp on the pad near the well and then ride the geyser up to the balcony on the left to get a blue star for upgrading your tool.

> Get the lamp before the other players and use it to get to places with coins and other goodies. If someone else gets it first, wait until they use it, then pick it up from the round pad and use it at another spot for your own personal gain.

Now carry the lamp over to the right and place it on the round pad to open the curtain. If the enemies have built a barrier, use a slam attack to break it down.

GEM

Go back to the fire-eater and drag him up the steps to the next area. Place him on the red pad so he burns a cage and reveals the first gem.

Jump down into the lower area and drag the sword swallower onto the blue pad to open the sword barrier.

Move the sword swallower up the steps and onto another blue pad to open a curtain, revealing a snake charmer.

> The Fodder here like to build barriers in front of the curtains to prevent you from getting inside these buildings. Use a slam attack to break down the barriers.

GEM

Take the snake charmer to the green pad on the right and then climb up the rope to get to the second gem.

GEM

To get the third gem and unlock concept art, drag the sword swallower down to the first area and place him on the blue pad in front of building where the lamp was. This opens the sword barrier for you.

EXTINGUISH THE HOT COALS

Move the snake charmer onto the green pad on the area's right side and then climb up the rope to the balcony.

Stand on the footprint pad and press the Use button to pull on the handle. This releases water onto the hot coals and opens the exit.

EXIT THE LEVEL

Challenge

After releasing the water, an arcade game appears near the snake charmer. Use it to play a challenge for coins and glory.

Finally, head through the exit to get to the next level.

Level 3

LEGEND

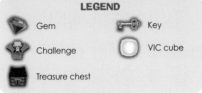

- Gem
- Challenge
- Treasure chest
- Key
- VIC cube

- Collectibles: 3 gems
- Guests to Rescue: 2

Disney TRIVIA

Agrabah is based on and designed after the medieval city of Baghdad.

GET THE LAMP

Walk over to the right to find the snake charmer. Drag him to the green pad on the left. Climb up the rope to get to the rooftop where you find the lamp.

Fight off the enemies on the rooftop and destroy the cobra statues that fire at you. There is a VIC cube up there if you feel the need for powering up. Once rooftop is clear, pick up the lamp.

USE THE LAMP TO TRANSFORM THINGS

GEM

Drop back down to the street and place the lamp on the pad near the well. Ride the geyser up to get to the balcony where you can find some coins and a gem.

Now take the lamp to the right and place it on a pad near the curtain so that you can get to the sword swallower.

SWALLOW THE SWORDS

GEM

Take the sword swallower all the way to the left side of the level and place him on the blue pad to clear the sword barrier so that you can get the second gem.

Now use the sword swallower to open the sword barrier at the stairs so you can get to the other side of the level.

COMPLETE THE ACROBATIC DISPLAY

Drag the sword swallower up the steps and onto a blue pad to release the acrobat. Now

you have to fight lots of enemies, including a Brute. Luckily, there is a VIC cube right there for you to use. While you are fighting, move around the area and destroy all the cobra statues.

Go back to the first area and bring the snake charmer to the green pad by the hot coals. Climb up the rope to get to the key on the balcony. Take the key to the chest on the right side of the level, next to the musical instrument booth, and get a blue star to upgrade your tool.

GEM

Take the lamp to the pad by the musical instrument booth and change it into a giant pipe organ. Play the colored notes that can be found above the door on the far right side of the level to open the door. Get the gem inside and unlock some character models.

Go back to the building by the snake charmer and get the acrobat. Move him over to the left and onto a gray pad.

Now go to the organ and play the colored notes above the door next to the hot coals to reveal another acrobat. As you do this, Jafar appears and starts raining down hot coals on you. Quickly get the acrobat over to the gray pad to complete the acrobatic display.

EXTINGUISH THE HOT COALS

Stand on the footprint pad by the acrobats and press the Use button to climb up them and get to the balcony.

Now move onto another footprint pad and pull on the handle to release water onto the hot coals.

FREE THE GUEST

Challenge

Once the hot coals have been extinguished, an arcade machine appears. Use it to play a challenge.

Finally, free the guest to complete the level and unlock the Sam costume.

Complete the Streets of Agrabah again and rescue another guest to unlock the Rapunzel costume.

Disney TRIVIA

The story of Aladdin originally comes from the classic *1001 Arabian Nights*.

AGRABAH PALACE

Level 1

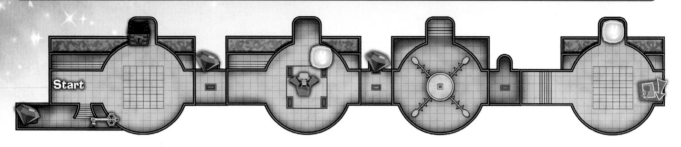

LEGEND

💎	Gem	🗝	Key
👕	Challenge	⬤	VIC cube
📦	Treasure chest	📑	Exit

- Collectibles: 3 gems
- Guests to Rescue: 0

UNCOVER THE PICTURE

At the start, move to the right and start fighting against the enemies. It is easier to complete your objective when the area is clear.

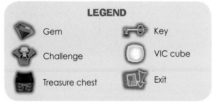

GEM

Walk to the front and then along the walkway to the left. Jump onto the cushion to bounce up and get the first gem.

Now it is time to work on the picture. Each tile changes when you touch it. Walk across the patterned side of the tiles to change them to the picture side. Then jump over the tiles with the picture side up so you don't turn them back to the pattern side by stepping on them a second time. Once the picture is complete, the door to the right opens. Move through the doorway to the next large area.

Pick up the key near the front of the area, then take it to the back, where a chest is waiting. Open it to upgrade your tool with a blue star.

LIGHT THE LAMPS

In this room, you must light four lamps. However, first deal with the enemies. When they are gone, drag the fire-eater onto one of the red pads so he can light the first lamp.

No sooner does he light the lamp than enemies appear and attack. Furthermore, they try to get to the green lever, which extinguishes all the flames in the lamps. Defeat them and then start moving the fire-eater around to light the lamps.

> When the enemies arrive, stay near the lever and guard it. Use slam attacks to keep them back—especially if your tool is upgraded with an area effect.

Eventually, a Roto appears and attacks. Stay out of its way and throw bombs at him. There is also a VIC cube in the back corner that you can pick up for a power-up. Once all the enemies are defeated, move the fire-eater around to light the remaining lamps, which opens the next set of doors to the right.

Challenge

After all the lamps are lit, an arcade game appears in the center of the room. Stop by and use it to play a challenge. Extra coins always come in handy for purchasing new costumes to wear.

GEM

Drag the fire-eater into the small room to the left and put him on the red pad. After he lights the bowl held by the elephant statue, a gem appears for you to collect. Now head to the right into the next large room.

SWALLOW THE SWORDS

In the next room, four sharp bars spin around a central platform. If these bars hit you, you are dead. As soon as one passes by, quickly move toward the right and jump up onto the platform. Step on the red switch to slow down the bars' speed.

Now run out and stand on the switch to slow the bars down again. Then go get the sword swallower and drag him around to the doorway on the right side.

While the bars are moving slowly, drag the sword swallower around to the small room on the left and out of danger.

Place the sword swallower on the blue pad to remove the barrier, then stand on the footprint pad and press the Use button to pull down on the handle to open the door to the right. Go through the door into another large room.

GEM

Place the sword swallower on the blue pad in the room on the left to remove the sword barrier. Then drag the fire-eater onto the red pad to make the third gem appear and unlock some music.

UNCOVER THE PICTURE

Before you can begin working on the picture, you have to clear out the enemies and then pull on the green levers to lower the spears in the areas where they are poking up through the floor. If you don't get rid of the enemies, they keep pulling the levers again to raise the spears.

The enemies aren't the only ones who can raise the spears. Wait until the other players are out of the picture and then pull a green lever yourself. They will get the point . . . in the end.

A good way to uncover these pictures, especially a large one like this is to start in the middle and work your way out. Try to do complete rows, jumping over those tiles that already have the picture side up.

EXIT THE LEVEL

As you start stepping on tiles to uncover the picture, more enemies show up, so take time to deal with them before continuing. Defeat the second wave. It stays clear for you to walk and jump on the picture to flip the patterned side over to the picture side. When the picture is complete, the exit opens.

Now walk through the exit to continue on to the next level in the palace.

Level 2

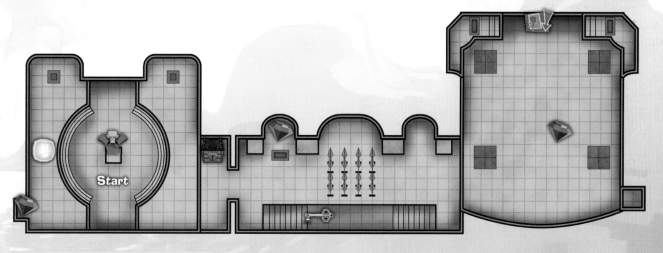

LEGEND

Gem	Key
Challenge	VIC cube
Treasure chest	Exit

- Collectibles: 3 gems
- Guests to Rescue: 0

EXPLORE THE PALACE

You begin in a large room with a cobra statue in the center. Walk around, picking up coins. However, if you move toward the steps, swords drop down and block your way.

SURVIVE THE ENEMY ATTACK

Jafar arrives and summons lots of Fodder to attack. Use slam attacks to cause area damage so that you can hurt several enemies at the same time.

After you defeat the first wave, Jafar fires energy beams and summons more Fodder as well as a Bulldog. Use the skills you have developed in previous worlds to defeat all the enemies.

UNCOVER THE PICTURE

Now tiles appear on the floor. You have to flip some of them over to make a picture. However, the cobra statue is now a sharp bar that spins around. Jump over it to avoid getting hit. Complete the picture and the cobra disappears. The swords that were blocking you in now form steps on the right side.

When Jafar fires a red beam at the cobra statue, the bar changes direction. As it slows down and then begins spinning in the opposite direction, quickly get out on the tiles since you have more time. Then as the bar starts coming toward you, move to the outside edge and jump over it. Wait until the next change in direction, then flip some more tiles.

Challenge

After you complete the picture, an arcade game appears in the center of the room. Use it to play a challenge.

GEM

Look in a little alcove on the room's left side to find the first gem.

Climb up the sword steps and continue into the next room. Pick up the key in the lower area at the front and go back by the sword steps to find the chest. Unlock it and upgrade your tool with the blue star inside.

Go back to the area where the key was and pull the green lever. This lowers the spears for a short amount of time. Quickly run up the steps and get to the footprint pad in the center. Pull on the lever to open the door to the right. When enemies appear, defeat them and destroy any traps they build because you'll be coming back here again.

UNCOVER THE PICTURES

In the next room, it all looks clear until you begin to move across it. Swords drop down and form a maze that is built as you go. In each corner of the maze, you must uncover a four-tile picture.

GEM

A gem is waiting in the middle of the maze. Work your way around to get to it. Or you can just uncover all the pictures and pick it up at the end.

After you finish with the last picture, all the swords fly away and the exit at the far end of this room opens up.

EXIT THE LEVEL

GEM

Before you exit, drag the fire-eater into the room with the spears and the handle. Place him on the red pad to light the bowl and make the third gem appear.

Finally, walk through the blue exit to advance to the final level in the *Aladdin* world.

Level 3

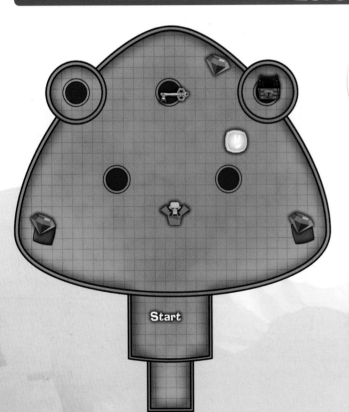

Start

LEGEND

 Gem   Key

Challenge   VIC cube

Treasure chest

- Collectibles: 3 gems
- Guests to Rescue: 2

DEFEAT JAFAR

GEM

This level is a boss battle and it takes place in the same area. At the start, rush over to the left side of the area and jump onto the cushion to bounce up and get the first gem.

Jafar starts the battle by sending some Fodder to attack. Defeat them with your own attacks and keep an eye on Jafar.

GEM

While Jafar is trans-
forming into a giant
cobra, rush to the right
side and bounce up from
a cushion to get a second
gem.

Jafar sends a Bulldog and more enemies to attack
while his snake's head returns to his body. Use a VIC
cube if you need it for a power-up.

Jafar pops up through several different circles in this
area. Get in close and start attacking the snake's body
while he fires his laser eyes.

Although you are in close so that the
laser blasts can't hit you, the shock
waves they create can still cause harm.
Be sure to jump over the shock waves
and then continue attacking.

Jafar has surrounded the snake body with swords
to prevent you from attacking. However, he keeps
blasting away with the laser eyes.

After you destroy one section of the snake's body, the
head flies up into the air and then moves across the
room, firing the laser eyes. Jump over the lasers as they
pass by. Also pick up the key that appears in the middle
of the room and take it to the chest in the back-right
corner to get a blue star that upgrades your tool.

There are five four-tile pictures on the floor. Each time
you uncover a picture, one of the holes through which
Jafar appears loses its sword barrier. Quickly uncover all
five pictures to resume the attack on the giant cobra.

Only two body segments are left. Keep hitting with your strongest attacks. Combine backhands with slam attacks. As Jafar moves to other holes, follow him.

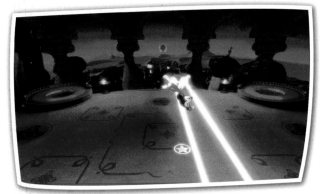

Destroy a second body segment and the cobra's head flies off again. Jump over the eyes' laser beams as it goes back and forth.

You now face another Bulldog and some Fodder. Defeat them and then focus on the snake again.

Once again, Jafar has surrounded his holes with swords. However, this time, you must uncover a large picture to remove all of them. In addition, he keeps firing lasers at you.

> If you lose all of your health while on the picture, you flip over tiles where you fall. Therefore, when you see the cobra charging up for a laser attack, move off the puzzle and then continue flipping tiles again after the shock wave passes. After the picture is uncovered, the swords fly away again.

Only one body segment remains. Keep hitting it and following Jafar where ever he goes.

Disney TRIVIA

Disney's Aladdin: A Musical Spectacular, a musical based on the movie, was created for and shown at Disney's California Adventure at the Hyperion Theater.

FREE THE GUEST

GEM

The final Gem can be found out in the open, near the top right corner of the battle area. Examine the circular platform near the top right, where Jafar pops out and you'll find the Gem ready to be claimed. Just be sure to grab it while Jafar is not attacking.

As that last body segment is destroyed, the Jafar cobra falls to pieces.

Challenge

Just as soon as you have defeated Jafar, an arcade game appears in the center of the room. Play a challenge for some more coins and bragging rights.

Finally, walk up and release the guest. Doing so unlocks the Aladdin costume.

Complete Agrabah Palace again and rescue a second guest to unlock the Jafar costume.

HERO OF THE SANDS
Complete the *Aladdin* world to earn this award.

ABANDONED EARTH

Level 1

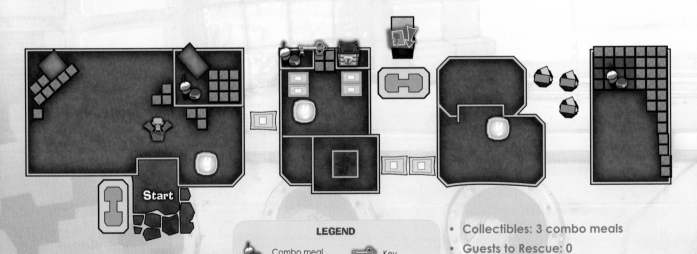

Start

LEGEND

Combo meal		Key	
Challenge		VIC cube	
Treasure chest		Exit	

- Collectibles: 3 combo meals
- Guests to Rescue: 0

START UP THE LIFT

The *WALL-E* world begins on Earth. Humans have long since abandoned the planet, leaving robots to clear up the mess the people left behind.

Many of the machines on earth require power from power blocks. Start by moving the power block to the socket to start the lift. Once it is working, use the lift to get to the upper area.

POWER UP THE MAGNET

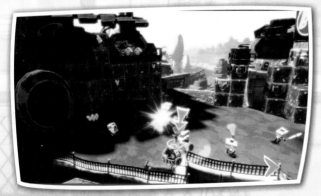

When you get to the upper area, several enemies attack. Fight them off and watch for them to throw bombs at you.

I have left you a VIC block at the front-right side of this area. It may come in handy for a power-up.

COMBO MEAL

Pick up one of the bombs that comes out of the pipes and throw it at the red trash blocks on the right side. When they blow up, a cage with a combo meal drops down. Throw another bomb at it and then collect it.

Blow up all the red trash blocks on the right side and then use the remaining blocks to jump up to the platform. Move the power block down to the ground and plug it into the socket on the right. The Fodder like to build a barrier in front of the socket, so use a bomb to clear away the barrier.

While the other players are fighting enemies or getting the power block, throw bombs at the red trash blocks on the left and then climb up the other blocks to get some coins. This also releases more Fodder that are stuck in cages in some of the blocks.

Challenge

As soon as you plug the power block into the socket, an arcade game appears just to the left. Be sure to stop by and use it to play a challenge.

GET ACROSS THE OIL SLICK

The power block starts up a magnet that raises a platform over the oil slick. Jump onto the platform and then to the right to the next area. There, you must fight against more enemies. Use the VIC block here for a power-up.

COMBO MEAL

Use the arrow switches to move the magnet to the right and then back to lift two platforms so that you can jump up and get your second combo meal. While you are there, pick up the key as well.

Walk back to the arrow switches and move the magnet to the right to raise a couple more platforms. Take the key to the chest and get a blue star for upgrading your tool. This also causes a lot of enemies to appear, so hurry and upgrade so that you have more power when you fight.

Next, move the magnet to the front and to the right to lift up two platforms over another oil slick. Get across the platforms to the other side.

BRING UP THE PLATFORM

Fight off more enemies to clear this area so that you can use the magnet trolley. This drives just like a cannon. However, when you press the Attack button, it attracts bombs. Then, when you release the button, it launchers the bombs—just like a cannon shot.

COMBO MEAL

Jump onto the bouncy barrels to get over to the far-right area. Throw bombs at the red trash blocks to get the third combo meal at the back and unlock some music.

Climb onto the trolley and use its magnet to attract bombs from the platform on the right. Launch them at the red trash blocks blocking the crank. This also releases a few Fodder trapped in some of the blocks, so get off the trolley and fight them. Once the crank is free, more enemies appear to try to stop you. Defeat them all.

Once it is clear, turn the crank to raise a platform and open the exit.

EXIT THE LEVEL

Now jump over onto the platform and from there, jump to the exit to continue to the next level on the Abandoned Earth.

Disney TRIVIA

WALL-E is the first Pixar movie to include live action scenes.

Level 2

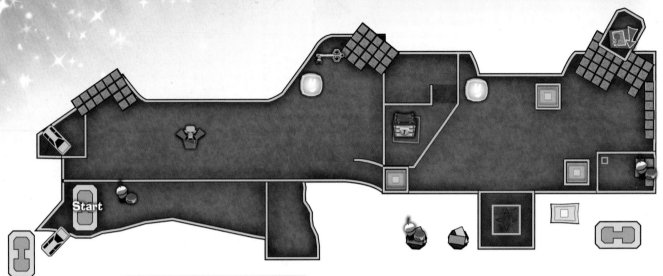

LEGEND

Combo meal   Key

Challenge   VIC cube

Treasure chest   Exit

- Collectibles: 3 combo meals
- Guests to Rescue: 0

START UP THE LIFT

At the start of this level, hit some trash to the left to reveal a red switch. Step on it to raise a platform to the left, then jump over to it to get some large coins.

Now move the gas remover to the right to clear the poisonous green gas from this area.

After you defeating several enemies that appear once the green gas is gone, move the power block to the socket on the left to power the lift.

COMBO MEAL

Before leaving the starting, low area, move into the open sewer tunnel. Go all the way to the back, turn left, and then come forward to get the first combo meal. Get out of the tunnel the same way you got in.

USE THE LASER TURRET

Get to the upper part of this area using the lift. Fight off a lot of enemies that come to attack. After they are gone, take control of the laser turret and use it to destroy the red trash blocks on the left side.

REPAIR THE SECOND LASER TURRET

Now climb up some stone blocks and move through some cages to get to another laser cannon. Move it down from the platform to the ground level and drag it over to the turret to the right of the first laser turret.

DESTROY THE BLOCKS

As soon as the laser is on the turret, you face a new enemy—the Spawner. You must defeat this new mini-boss as well as the other enemies that appear.

Spawner

The Spawner is the fourth mini-boss. It gets its name from its ability to send Fodder to attack you. In addition, it can fire large fireballs. When you see its cannon charging up, getting ready to fire, be ready to press the Use button as the fireball gets close to you. This hits the fireball back at the Spawner and stuns it. Now you can move in to attack without worrying about getting hurt. The Spawner also attacks by sitting on you or bumping into you to knock you off a platform.

🏆 **TIME FOR A DIET!**
Defeat your first Spawner to receive this award.

Challenge

Defeat the Spawner to make an arcade machine appear in the middle of this area. Use it to play a challenge and earn some coins and glory.

Now use the second laser turret to destroy the red trash blocks. This creates some steps you can jump up to get onto the higher platform. Be sure to pick up the key on the ground level before moving on.

Take the key to the upper platform and open the chest to get a blue star and upgrade your tool.

CONTROL THE MAGNET

Drop down to the lower level on the right. Carefully avoid the green gas and find the arrow switches. Move the magnet to the right to raise a platform.

COMBO MEAL

Jump to the left onto a couple of bouncy barrels to get the second combo meal.

Climb up on the platform and jump up to a platform on the right. Move the gas remover off this platform and clear the green gas to find a laser turret.

COMBO MEAL

Jump back up to the platform on the right. Step on the red switch, then stand on the arrow platform; it shoots you up to the top of some blocks, where you can get a third combo meal and unlock some concept art for your efforts.

Move the magnet to the right of the arrow switches to raise a platform so that you can get to another platform with some large coins.

Use the laser turret to shoot the red trash blocks along the back wall. After they are destroyed, a mini-boss and enemies attack. Use bombs and your weapon to defeat them all.

USE THE MAGNET TO ESCAPE

Now move the magnet to the back of the area to lift a platform and open the exit.

EXIT THE LEVEL

Now jump up onto the platform and continue up onto some blocks to get to the exit. Go through it to get to the next level.

Level 3

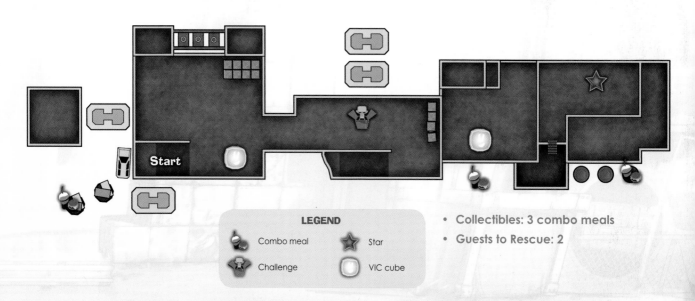

LEGEND

Combo meal

Challenge

Star

VIC cube

• Collectibles: 3 combo meals

• Guests to Rescue: 2

POWER UP THE PLATFORM

COMBO MEAL

From the start, jump over to a bouncy barrel and then jump again to another barrel to get the first combo meal.

Move out onto the main area and defeat a large wave of enemies that attack. Be sure to pick up a VIC cube near the front of the area for a power-up.

When the area is clear, climb onto one of the magnet trolleys and attract a bomb to you. Aim at the targets at the back of the area and launch bombs to flip parts of an old street sign over to form a bridge. Also launch bombs at the red trash blocks to the right to clear a path in that direction.

Climb up the blocks on the right side and then jump across the bridge sections to get to the power block on the left side. Move the power block off the platform and plug it into the socket to power up the platform.

USE THE GAS REMOVER

As the platform rises, a Spawner and more enemies appear. Focus on defeating the Spawner first by hitting the fireballs back at it and then moving in to attack while it is stunned.

After defeating all of the enemies, jump across the platform to get to the gas remover. Move it across the platform and keep going to the right.

REMOVE THE DEADLY GAS

Continue all the way to the next barrier of blocks, using the gas remover to get rid of the green gas. Once this is done, defeat the mini-boss that appears and any other enemies.

DESTROY THE BLOCKS

Challenge

As soon as you defeat the mini-boss, an arcade game appears. Stop by and play a challenge to get some more coins.

Go back to the left to get a magnet trolley and drive it to the right. Launch bombs at the red trash blocks to clear a way to the right.

> Launch bombs at the red trash blocks at the back of the area. Then jump across to the platform to get some large coins.

COMBO MEAL

Pick up and throw bombs at the blocks on a lower level near the front of the area. Blow up the trash blocks and break open a cage to release a combo meal. Then jump across and pick it up.

Climb up the ladder to the final area and fight the enemies. Go to the right to find a green lever. Pick it up and carry it to the slot by the door on the left. Use the handle to open the door and reveal a socket. Now plug the power block into the socket.

SHOOT THE GREEN BLOCKS

Walk over to the laser turret and start shooting the green blocks. You need to get thirty points to complete this task. Each green box you hit is worth 30 points.

> Don't hit the red blocks. If you do, bombs fly out and land near you. Get off the turret to avoid the explosion if this happens and then get back on again to keep shooting.

FREE THE GUEST

COMBO MEAL

Step on the red switch at the front of the final area to make three sewer doors open to form platforms. Drop through a gap on the left side of a chain-link barrier and jump across the platforms to get the combo meal. Then, quickly jump back across to the left before the timer is up and the doors close. Getting this third combo meal unlocks some character models.

Finally, rescue the guest and unlock the Celia costume as your reward.

> Play through Abandoned Earth again and save a second guest to unlock the Abu costume.

AXIOM BELOWDECKS
Level 1

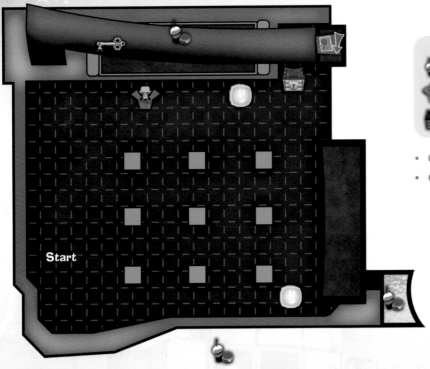

LEGEND

	Combo meal		Key
	Challenge		VIC cube
	Treasure chest		Exit

- Collectibles: 3 combo meals
- Guests to Rescue: 0

DISNEP TRIVIA

WALL-E stands for Waste Allocation Load Lifter-Earth-class. EVE stands for Extraterrestrial Vegetation Evaluator.

MOVE THE SECURITY BOTS

Now that you have boarded the *Axiom*, you must manipulate the guide tracks on the floor to complete your objectives

The security bots act to block the green tracks. Start off by moving all three security bots to the three positions in the middle, so that all the tracks from the left now go to the middle door at the back of the area.

GUIDE THE ROBOTS TO THE DOORS

A number appears on the sign above the middle door. This is how many robots you need to get to that door. A space ship arrives and begins unloading robots. The robots will follow the tracks and go to the door. This first group is easy because there are no enemies to mess with the process. It is important to get the robots to the doors in order to raise sections of a light track up above the doors so that you can get to the exit.

As soon as the first door is filled with the required number of robots, enemies appear and start attacking. Strop them from building traps and clear them out as quickly as possible. They are sent to stop you from getting incoming robots to the correct doors.

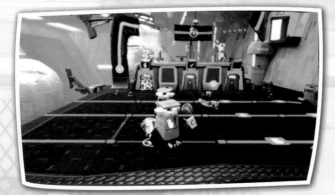

Once you get most of the enemies cleared out, move the security bots to the left to change the tracks so they lead into the door on the left.

The security bot nearest the doors is the most important. If the enemies move it, none of the robots from the space ship can get to the correct door.

Although getting the first door filled with robots was easy, the enemy is not going to make it easy the second time. In addition to attacking you, some of the Fodder move the security bots off their positions to prevent the robots from getting to the doors. Stand guard near the security bots and attack any enemies who get close. Slam attacks work great since they can knock enemies away from you and the security bots.

COMBO MEAL

When you get a chance, step on the red switch at the front of the area to raise two platforms. Drop down and get the combo meal and some coins, then quickly jump back up to the main area before the timer runs out and the platforms move away.

Each time a new space ship arrives, check to see to which door those robots are supposed to go. A number appears over the door a little before the ship

arrives. Quickly move the security bots into the correct position so that the tracks lead to the correct door. Enemies are constantly trying to stop you.

It can be tough to try to make sure all three security bots stay in position. Therefore, concentrate on the two closest to the door and defend them. There are enough robots unloaded onto those two tracks to fill the door.

Be careful with power-ups and slam attacks. They not only defeat the enemies, but also these attacks can destroy the robots you are trying to get to the doors.

COMBO MEAL

Move a security bot over to a far-right position to activate a light track. Then stand on the footprint pad and press the Use button to climb up the light track to get onto a walkway. Step on the red switch and then jump down to get the combo meal before the door closes.

After two doors have been filled, a mini-boss and more enemies attack. Concentrate on defeating them and forget about the robots for now.

Challenge

As soon as the second door is filled and the mini boss arrives, an arcade game appears. Get to it as quickly as you can to play a challenge. It disappears as soon as the next space ship arrives. While a challenge is activated, the rest of the game pauses, so don't worry about the mini-boss and other enemies. They return after the challenge is complete.

Keep defending those security bots so that you can get the last robots into the final door and complete your objective.

CLIMB THE LIGHT TRACK AND EXIT THE LEVEL

COMBO MEAL

Stand on the footprint pad at the area's far-left corner and press the Use button to begin climbing it. Follow it along to the middle to get the combo meal and unlock some music.

Get back up onto the light track and follow it all the way to the exit to begin the next level.

Drop down from the light track onto a platform above the doors and pick up the key. Carry it over to the chest in the back-right corner and open it to get a blue star for upgrading your tool.

Level 2

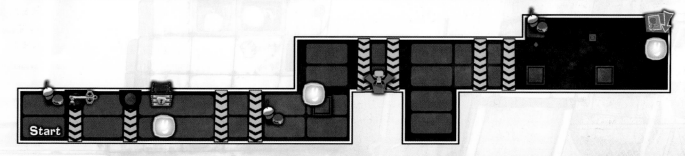

LEGEND

 Combo meal   Key

 Challenge   VIC cube

 Treasure chest   Exit

- Collectibles: 3 combo meals
- Guests to Rescue: 0

POWER UP THE DOOR

In this first area, two laser beams fire down the length of the floor. Jump over one to get to the green lever and pull it.

Watch for the small doors to open at the back of the area. This gives you a warning that the lasers are about to activate.

As gravity reverses, the key and power block on high platforms all go to the ceiling—you do, too. Move the key and the power block toward the front of the area so that when you switch gravity back to normal, it falls to the floor and not back onto the platform.

COMBO MEAL

While you are on the ceiling, walk over to the left to pick up the first combo meal. Then pull the green lever to drop back down to the floor.

Pick up the key from the ground and use it to unlock the chest to get to the blue star inside. Your tool is now upgraded.

Pull the power block over to the socket to open the door on the right side. Then move into the next area.

RELEASE THE POWER BLOCK

As soon as you enter the next area, enemies appear and attack. Defeat them and then move to the back wall and pull the green lever.

Watch out for the two fans located between the green levers. If you move in front of them, they will blow you off the platform.

When you pull on the green lever, gravity reverses. Walk across the ceiling to the right and pull the crank over to the left side.

COMBO MEAL

While on the ceiling, continue to the left side to get the second combo meal.

Pull on the green lever on the left to change gravity back to normal. Once you're on the ground, drag the crank to its slot and turn it to raise a platform to the right.

Challenge

As you raise the platform, an arcade game appears on the platform. Use it to play a challenge.

Once the platform is raised, the door near the left green lever opens. Now you can get the power block. Drag it over to the right and place it in the socket to open the door on the right so you can get to the next area.

MAKE A POWER BLOCK

In the final area, jump over a couple of lasers and then start moving blocks into a trash compactor. There are three red lights on the compactor. Each time you put a block into the compactor, a red light turns green.

After the first block is in the compactor, a mini-boss and some more enemies appear. There is a VIC cube on the right side of the area, so grab it for a power-up to help you defeat the enemies.

Move two more blocks into the compactor and then step on the red switch to create a power block from the three blocks of trash.

Drag the power block out of the compactor and insert it into the socket on the right to open the exit.

EXIT THE LEVEL

COMBO MEAL

Drag the jump cannon from the right side over to the platform on the left. Jump into the cannon and then launch yourself up onto the platform to get the third combo meal and unlock some concept art.

As the exit opens, enemies appear. Fight them if you want to, then move through the exit to advance to the next level.

Disney TRIVIA

Everyday WALL-E watches a video of the classic musical *Hello, Dolly!*

Level 3

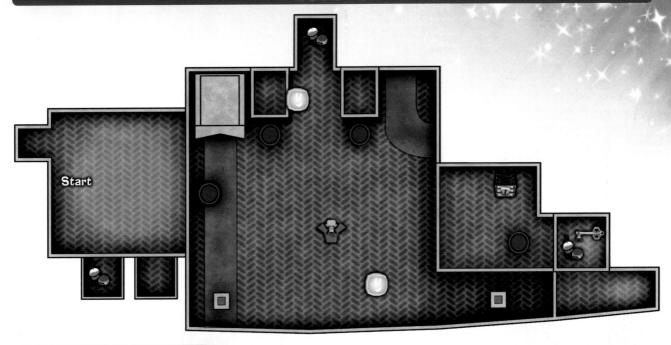

Start

LEGEND

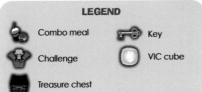

Combo meal

Challenge

Treasure chest

Key

VIC cube

- Collectibles: 3 combo meals
- Guests to Rescue: 2

USE THE TRASH COMPACTOR

As you enter this level, drop down to the main floor and defeat the first wave of enemies that attack you.

COMBO MEAL

Step on the red switch in the front-left corner of the area to raise a couple of platforms. Then jump onto these platforms to get the first combo meal.

Don't pull on the green lever on the left side. This opens an air lock and everything in the room gets sucked out into space—blocks, enemies, players, keys. Of course, you can always pull the lever and move to the front-left corner—while all the other players are sucked from the area.

Move three blocks into the trash compactor and then step on the red switch to create a power block.

Now drag the power block under the smasher and onto a lift that carries you up to a platform. Put the power block into the socket.

A mini-boss and other enemies appear and try to stop you. Pick up the VIC cube by the trash compactor and use the power-up to defeat all the enemies.

The enemies try to build a cannon down below that can fire at you on the upper platform. Pick up bombs on this platform and throw them down at the cannon to destroy it. You can also throw the bombs down on other players as well.

Challenge

Move the power block to the area's front-right corner. Step on the red switch to temporarily stop a smasher so you can pass underneath it.

As soon as you plug the power block into the socket, an arcade game appears in the center of the area. Be sure to play a challenge to win some more coins.

Pull on the green lever to open a door containing some big coins on the other side of the smasher.

MAKE A JUMP CANNON

A second trash compactor moves out into the level when you put the power block into the socket. Drop down to the main floor and move three trash blocks into the compactor. Step on the red switch and the compactor turns them into a jump cannon.

Carry the key to the nearby chest and open it to get a blue star. Upgrade your tool once again.

SHUT DOWN THE FURNACE

Another mini-boss and enemies appear. Use the second VIC cube, located near the front of the area, and power up your attacks. Some bombs at the front of the area work great on the mini-boss.

Move the jump cannon down to the main floor and position it in one of the slots by the furnace. Use the cannon to jump up to a small platform and pull a green lever.

COMBO MEAL

Move the jump cannon under the smasher and up the lift to the platform on the right. Use it to jump up to a smaller, higher platform, where you can get the second combo meal—as well as a key.

Quickly drop down and move the jump cannon to the other side. Jump up to the other platform and pull the second green lever before the timer runs out. This shuts down the furnace.

FREE THE GUEST

COMBO MEAL

Now that the furnace is cooled down, move inside it to collect the third combo meal and unlock some character models.

Finally, free the guest and unlock the Tinkerbell costume as a reward for your hard work.

Play through *Axiom* Belowdecks again to rescue a second guest and unlock the Robin Hood costume.

AXIOM CAPTAIN'S DECK

Level 1

LEGEND

- Combo meal
- Challenge
- Treasure chest
- Key
- VIC cube
- Exit

- Collectibles: 3 combo meals
- Guests to Rescue: 0

BL

Start

POWER THE LIFT

You have made it onto the main deck of the *Axiom*. This level is a large area with lots of things to do.

Start by moving to the middle of the area and dragging the power block to the socket in the back wall. The provides power to the red switch on the left side.

After defeating the enemies that appear, step on the red switch to shut off the reddish energy field so that you can get to another socket and a key.

Carry the key to the chest on the right side near the first socket. Open the chest to get a blue star to upgrade your tool.

COMBO MEAL

Drag the passenger over to the side and jump onto the passenger. You bounce up high. Land on the upper walkway and get a combo meal.

While the other players are going after the power blocks, grab a passenger and start bouncing up to higher areas to collect coins before other people do.

The second power block is behind the combo meal. Move it down to the main deck and then put it into the socket underneath the upper walkway on the left.

The enemy like to build traps and a barrier near the lift. Try to defeat them before they complete these structures.

COMBO MEAL

Move the passenger or the Captain over to the right side and jump on the bouncy person to get up to another walkway where the second combo meal can be found.

COMBO MEAL

After getting back down to the main deck, move the passenger or Captain to the right and jump up to another higher area. Step on the red switch and then quickly stand on the round pad, which springs you up into the air to get the third combo meal and unlocks some music.

While you are up on the higher level, get the power block and drag it down to the main deck. Plug it into the nearby socket.

More enemies appear, so fight them off. The last power block supplies energy to a nearby red switch. Step on it to raise a platform with a green lever on it. Carry the lever over to the slot by the power block and then pull it to redirect the power toward the lift.

Now walk over to the crank and turn it so that the power from the third power block moves to the lift. Also pull the green lever by the first power block so that three streams of energy are all going to the lift.

USE THE CAPTAIN TO ESCAPE

A mini-boss and several enemies appear. There are a couple VIC cubes in the area which you can use for power-ups to help defeat these enemies.

After the area is clear again, move the Captain onto the lift. Ride it up to the upper level, then drag him to the right and place him into the control console to open the exit.

EXIT THE LEVEL

Now all that remains is to walk through the exit to get to the next level.

Disney TRIVIA

Throughout the movie, characters or items from other Pixar movies can be seen in the trash on the Earth or in the baskets in WALL-E's home. Look for Hamm and Rex as well as Lightning McQueen.

Level 2

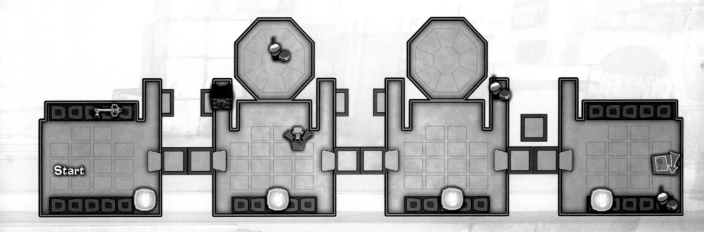

Start

LEGEND

🍔	Combo meal	🔑	Key	
⚙	Challenge	⬜	VIC cube	
📦	Treasure chest	📄	Exit	

- Collectibles: 3 combo meals
- Guests to Rescue: 0

SCAN THE BOOT

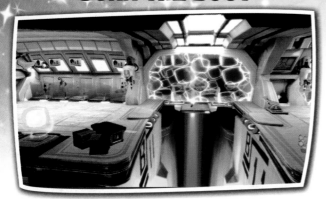

You must get through this corridor to reach the *Axiom's* bridge.

Walk over to the green lever and pull on it to lower the blue energy barriers along the back wall. Be ready for a fight because enemies appear. A VIC cube near the front of this area can provide a power-up.

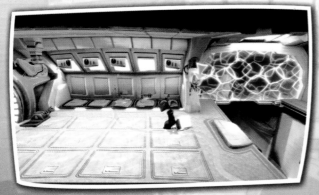

Drag the boot over to the scanner on the right side to lower a red energy field along the back of the area.

Grab the key and carry it to the back of the area. Jump across a gap to get to the chest on the other side. Open it to upgrade your tool with the blue star inside.

POWER UP THE ARM

Pull on the green lever to extend a bridge across the gap. Then go back and get the boot.

Drag the boot over to the scanner by the lever to open a room with a power block inside. Before you can do anything else, you must defeat the enemies that appear.

COMBO MEAL

Walk into the room and pick up the first combo meal.

Move the power block into the socket and then fight off the enemies that appear. They attempt to build a cannon in the left corner, so either stop them or destroy the cannon before it causes you a lot of damage. Notice the VIC cube in this area as well.

Now move the boot over to the arm on the left side. It carries the boot to another scanner, which then deactivates another energy field.

Challenge

An arcade game appears after the boot has been scanned. Stop by and use it to play a challenge and beat your friends, or just collect some extra coins.

ACTIVATE THE BRIDGE

Cross over the gap on the walkway and then fight the mini-boss and enemies that appear. A power-up from the VIC cube comes in handy.

There are bombs in several places in this level. Use them against mini-bosses and Fodder—and even other players. Target the one in the lead so you can catch up, or any other player to keep yourself in the lead.

Now move the boot over to the next scanner to release a green lever. Pick up the lever and place it in the slot and pull it to extend a bridge across the next gap.

LEAVE THE CORRIDOR

Drag the boot again—this time out onto the bridge—and place it under the scanner. Now walk to the right and step on the red switch to activate the scanner. It deactivates the energy field.

COMBO MEAL

Go back across the bridge and toward the back where there energy field was to get the second combo meal.

COMBO MEAL

Walk back across the bridge to the right and step on the red switch near the front of the area. Quickly walk onto the round pad and spring up to get the third combo meal and unlock concept art.

A power block is on another walkway at the back of the area—across the gap from the combo meal. Move it to the socket on the right side to power up the final scanner and cause another mini-boss and more enemies to appear. Use the VIC cube and defeat them all.

Once it is clear, drag the boot over to the last scanner, which opens the exit for you.

EXIT THE LEVEL

Now all that remains is for you to walk through the exit to get to the last level.

Level 3

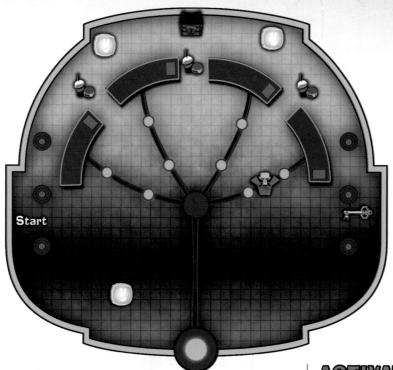

LEGEND

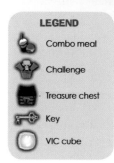

Combo meal

Challenge

Treasure chest

Key

VIC cube

- Collectibles: 3 combo meals
- Guests to Rescue: 2

GET INTO THE CAPTAIN'S DECK

Start by pressing the red button on the console to open the door to the Captain's deck. Walk through the door and get ready for the final battle.

ACTIVATE ALL THE CONSOLES

To activate a console, the power must be directed toward it and all nodes must be blue. The first console on the left is ready to activate, so press the red button on it.

Step on the red nodes to turn them blue, then turn the crank to direct power toward another console. Press the red button and then repeat the process to activate the remaining consoles so that all four are green.

Before you activate all of the consoles—and things get chaotic—or while the other players are doing the job for you, head to the right to find the key. Then take it to the back of the area where the chest is. An upgraded tool comes in handy during this battle.

DEFEAT THE BOSS

When all four consoles are activated, Auto, the ship's wheel tries to stop you. As this boss drops into the slot near the crank to deactivate the consoles, it is surrounded by lasers. A wave of enemies attacks, too, so fight them off.

After the consoles have been deactivated, the lasers around Auto turn off and the boss is vulnerable. Quickly get in close and hit the boss a few times.

When Auto is down in the socket, stay close to the lasers while you are fighting the Fodder. Then, as soon as the lasers disappear, turn your attacks onto Auto.

The four consoles must be activated again. Go step on the red nodes and then repeat the process from before: turning the crank and pressing red buttons. Auto has some small turrets that rise up from the floor and fire at you, so jump over the shots to avoid getting hit.

Auto lowers down into the slot again and then rotates around to try to hit you with a laser beam. Jump over the beam as you continue activating consoles. Auto makes an energy shock wave attack as well. Just jump over the shock wave to stay safe.

Once all the consoles are activated, watch out for the small turrets and get in close to attack Auto again.

COMBO MEAL

After attacking Auto, a combo meal appears to the right side. Pick it up and add it to your collection.

Auto tries a new attack. It activates two lasers on the sides of the room, then turns the ship to tilt the deck. If that were not enough, bombs come tumbling past you. Dodge the bombs and jump to avoid falling down into the laser on the lower side.

After the deck returns to level, a giant boxing glove starts pounding into the deck. Watch for the round shadow and jump out of the way before you get hit.

COMBO MEAL

After activating the consoles for the first time, this Combo Meal appears the top center of the room, between the two computer consoles. You can grab it as soon as it appears, but it's probably best to wait until the coast is clear to pick it up. You can even grab it once you've defeated Auto!

Keep activating the consoles again as you fight against enemies. Auto tilts the ship again and drops bombs, so just stay alive and working on the consoles.

Auto drops down again to deactivate the consoles. Wait for the lasers to disappear and then let the boss have it.

COMBO MEAL

After hitting Auto and defeating it, the third combo meal appears to the left. Pick it up and unlock character models.

FREE THE GUEST

Now that Auto has been defeated, you must take on the mini-boss that was helping Auto. Grab a VIC cube and go after the mini-boss and other enemies in the area to clear it.

Finally, release the guest from the block to unlock the WALL-E costume.

Challenge

Defeat the mini-boss to make an arcade game appear on the right side of the level. Take the time to play a challenge before continuing on.

Play through the *Axiom* Captain's Deck again and save a second guest to unlock the EVE costume.

RETURNING TO EARTH
Complete the *WALL-E* world and you get this award.

SAVIOUR OF THE UNIVERSE!
Complete all the worlds to earn this award.

COMPULSIVE COLLECTOR
Collect all the world collectables in the game to achieve this prestigious award

NAVIGATING THE UNIVERSE

The *Disney Universe* is a virtual world in which you are one of the guests. Unfortunately, after HEX took control, the *Disney Universe* is no longer a safe place. Several guest have been captured by HEX and his bot minions. If you are to get through the various worlds, you need to know how to avoid danger as well as how to fight against the enemies.

> There are six worlds in the *Disney Universe*. Each world has three locations. In turn, there are three levels for each location.

CONTROLLING YOUR CHARACTER

Since your character is how you interact with the *Disney Universe*, it is important to learn how to control your character.

> To quickly get into the game and learn the most important controls, play through the London location of the *Pirates of the Caribbean* world. The first level serves as a tutorial for playing the game.

> Since *Disney Universe* is available for several different gaming systems and controller settings, the specific controls vary. However, it doesn't matter what controls you use. You still aren't going to beat me and my army of bots.

Movement

WALKING/RUNNING

The basic way of getting around is by walking and running. Using an analog stick, you walk by applying a little pressure to the stick in the direction you want to move. Apply full pressure on the analog stick to make your character run. There really is no advantage to walking unless you are trying to get close to an edge without falling off. Therefore, you should run most of the time.

JUMPING

You can jump into the air while standing on any solid surface. Just press the Jump button and you jump straight up into the air. To jump to the side, for example, to jump up onto an object or across gaps, press the movement control in the direction you want to jump as you press the Jump button. You use jumping almost as much as you do walking.

DOUBLE-JUMP

At times you need to jump higher or farther. That calls for a double-jump. To perform a double-jump, jump up into the air and then press the Jump button again. Your character performs a flip in midair during a double-jump. When you have to jump across a wide distance, try a double-jump to make it all the way to the other side.

While your character respawns after falling off the edge of the playing area, you can drop or fall from any height as long as you land on solid ground without taking any damage. Lava, water, and other bodies of liquid do cause you to respawn if you fall or walk into them—unless you are a zombie, which can walk into and under water.

Interacting

Part of the fun in the *Disney Universe* is interacting with items, objects, enemies, and even other players. In most cases, you interact by pressing the Use button.

CARRYING

In many levels, you need to pick up small items such as keys, watches, swords, and so forth. Press the Use button to pick them up and then press the Use button again to set them down or use the item.

DRAGGING AND PUSHING

Some objects are too big to pick up. However, you can still move them around. To move such an object, stand next to it and hold down the Use button. You then drag or push the object as you move around. Release the button to stop moving the object.

HANGING

At times, you need to grab onto an object and hang from it as it moves across a gap or open area. There is often a pad of some type in the area where you can grab onto such an object as it moves past you. To hang onto an object, press the Use button and continue to hold it. Release the button to drop down from the moving object.

THROWING

Some items can be picked up, carried, and then thrown. These include bombs and water balloons. Press the Use button to pick up these items from a pile or basket, and then press the Attack button to throw the item in the direction you are facing.

> When carrying a bomb or water balloon, don't hold onto it for too long or it will explode if it is a bomb or burst if it is a water balloon. While the water from a water balloon won't hurt you, the explosion will.

At other times, turn cranks in one direction and then another to move objects back and forth or up and down. Turning a crank is easy. Just walk up to one and move around. As you move, your character automatically pushes against one of the arms of the crank and rotates it.

SWITCHES

It can't get much easier than interacting with a switch. Switches are red squares on the ground. To activate them, just walk or step onto a switch. Some switches have timers. They turn green while they are operational and then turn red again once the timer runs out. Switches can open doors, raise platforms, and do several other actions. Be sure to use switches whenever you see them because they often allow you to get to goodies. Some switches also appear on controls or consoles. For those, you must press the Use button to activate them.

PICKING UP ENEMIES AND PLAYERS

In addition to picking up items, you can also pick up and carry small enemies and even other players. Press the Use button to pick them up. Continue holding down the Use button if you want to spin them and then release to throw them. If you spin them too long, you get dizzy and just drop them.

> If another player picks you up, quickly press random buttons on your controller to break out of the hold.

LEVERS

Green levers appear in many levels. These act like switches in that they activate or open objects. To use a lever, walk up to it and press the Use button. If a lever can be used again, it stays green. Red levers can't be used. Levers can also have timers. While the timer is counting down, the lever is red. Then it turns back to green when it is usable.

CRANKS

Some objects do not require you to press the Use button. Cranks must be turned. In most cases, turn cranks clockwise to make something lift up or move.

Riding and Driving

ANIMALS

Several types of animals can be found throughout the worlds. They range from warthogs to donkeys to zebras.

Animals can be ridden by both players and enemies alike. Press the Use button to mount and dismount from an animal. While riding an animal, you move around just like you do on foot and can even jump. By pressing the Attack button, the animal performs its own unique attack. A donkey kicks at the target with its hind legs, a zebra attacks with its front legs, and a pig releases a green cloud of gas that temporarily stuns enemies as well as other players. While they are not as effective at combat—especially when fighting more than one enemy—animals can be fun to ride around a level.

VEHICLES

Some levels have vehicles that you can drive. They include cannons, snow mobiles, magnet trolleys, and even large rubber ducks—complete with their own cannon! Press the Use button to climb onto a vehicle and to get off. Push the movement control stick or pad in the direction you want the vehicle to go when moving and your character automatically turns it. Press the Attack button to fire the cannon or activate the magnet.

> While on a vehicle, enemies can still attack and damage you. Therefore, it is usually a good idea to get off the vehicle and clear out the enemies before using the vehicle.

FIGHTING

HEX is out to stop you from rescuing guests and has sent his bots to attack you. The only way to get through the levels in one piece is to fight back. No matter which costume you are wearing, you always have a tool that you can use to fight off enemies. It is important to know the types of attacks and combos you can perform when fighting.

> If you chain together several simple attacks, getting a hit with each one, your character performs a finishing move that inflicts more damage and it looks cool, too.

Combos

SIMPLE ATTACK

This swing with your tool causes some damage if you hit a target. Press the Attack button to perform a simple attack.

AIR ATTACK

Some enemies fly above the reach of your simple attack. Therefore, you need to jump up into the air to hit them.

To perform an air attack, press the Jump button while facing the enemy and then, while in midair, press the Attack button. This usually knocks a flying enemy down to the ground.

GROUND SLAM ATTACK

This is another combo that combines jumping and attacking. Perform a double-jump and while in midair, press and hold the Attack button. As you land, you slam your tool into the ground and cause more damage than normal to whatever you hit and also create a small shock wave that damages others nearby.

As you collect blue stars, your tool upgrades and gains extra powers, which are released by ground slam attacks. At level 2, your tool releases an electrical charge that shocks nearby enemies. Upgrade to level 3 and your tool now has a fire attack, causing more damage to the area as well as firing off small fireballs that damage whatever they hit—including you. Finally, upgrade again to level 4 and your tool has a magical attack that damages enemies in a larger radius.

Ground slam attacks are great for attacking enemies as well as other players. Plus, if another player just happens to be in the area when you are slamming an enemy, it will look like an accident.

UPPERCUT

Hold down the Attack button and after a brief pause, you perform an uppercut. This attack causes more damage than a simple attack and can hit more than one enemy since it has a wider swing.

UPPERCUT AND SLAM

When using an uppercut, continue to hold down the Attack button as you automatically jump up into the air. When you come down, you come down with a ground slam. This is a great attack when fighting lots of enemies all around you.

DODGE

When fighting against mini-bosses, a button icon appears on the screen as the mini-boss prepares for an attack. By pressing that button, you can dodge the attack and the mini-boss will be stunned temporarily because it missed you. This gives you the perfect opportunity to go after the mini-boss with your array of attacks and combos.

Health

When you get hit or take damage, you health meter appears as curved bars around the base of your character.

When the health bars all disappear, you respawn with a full health meter. As you defeat enemies, some leave behind red hearts. Collect these hearts to restore health bars. Respawning has a negative effect on your rating at the end of a location.

POWER-UPS

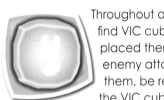

Throughout all of the levels you can find VIC cubes. VIC has strategically placed them in areas where the enemy attacks you—so if you see them, be ready for a fight. Most of the VIC cubes contain power-ups that give you an advantage over the enemy during a fight. However, HEX has included some curses, so you never know what you will get until you touch one of these cubes.

Power-ups and curses last only for a short amount of time—about 10 seconds. Therefore, use them while you can and don't pick them up until you need them during a fight.

Power-Ups

Name	Description
Bee Head	A beehive covers your head. Press the Attack button to shoot swarms of bees at targets.
Electric Punch	These boxing gloves give an electric sting when you punch enemies and other players.
Electric Ray Gun	This gun shoots out a bolt of electricity that zaps and defeats anyone it touches.
Electric Shield	A shield surrounds you and protects you from damage. Plus, anyone that touches the shield gets shocked.
Laser Ray	Fire laser beams from this gun to defeat enemies and other players.
Medusa	A mask appears over your head. Press the Attack button to turn players and enemies in front of you into stone statues that can be hit to destroy them.
Midas Touch	Hit others with your tool and they turn to gold. Hit them again and they turn into gold coins.
Money Magnet	You hold a large magnet that attracts coins from other players as well as the environment. You can't attack, but can get rich.
Money Maker	You turn into a jackhammer and drill coins out of the ground as you move around. While you can't make regular attacks, you can ground slam.
Plasma Gun	You get a gun that fires a burst of plasma. It takes only a single hit to defeat an enemy.
Power Punch	You get a pair of boxing gloves. Defeat enemies with a single hit while wearing these gloves.

Power-Ups (continued)

Name	Description
Shield	A magic barrier surrounds you and protects you from all damage.
Shooter	You get a gun that fires shots that defeat enemies with a single hit. Hold down the attack button for rapid fire.
Snowman	Your character turns into a snowman armed with a freeze ray gun that turns enemies and other players into blocks of ice.
Tool Modifier	Modifies your tool so that it defeats enemies and other players with a single hit.
Tornado	You turn into a whirlwind that damages anyone and anything that gets close as you move around the area.

Some power-ups and curses are not available in single-player games and appear only when playing against other players.

Curses

Name	Description
Basketball	You turn into a basketball that bounces around the area and can perform ground slam attacks.
Bomb Head	Your head turns into a bomb that explodes after several seconds. You can also press the Attack button to make the bomb explode when you want it to.
Chicken	You are transformed into a chicken. You can still attack others by pecking at them.
Dizzy Controls	A box is placed over your head and the controls are inverted for a short period of time.
Evil Boot	Stomp, you turn into a boot. Kick other players and enemies.
Fat Guy	Your character gets large and stomps the ground when jumping or attacking, which causes damage to nearby enemies and other players.
Hamburger Head	Your head turns into a hamburger. A pair of wind-up teeth appear and try to eat the hamburger. Stay away from them or you respawn.
Jack in the Box	You turn into a box with legs. Press the Attack button to spring the lid and reveal either a coin or a bomb.
Lightning Strike	A cloud forms over your head. If there is no one nearby, the lightning hits you. Get close to other players or enemies so the lightning hits them instead.
Monkey	You turn into a toy monkey. Use the big cymbals on your hands to attack enemies and other players.

GOODIES

Disney Universe is filled with lots of things for you to pick up and collect.

COINS

Coins are everywhere. They can be found just lying around. Smash some objects and more coins appear. You even get coins when you defeat enemies. Get as many coins as you can so that you can unlock new worlds and purchase new costumes that you have unlocked by rescuing guests.

BLUE STARS

Blue stars upgrade your tool for the costume you are currently wearing. They can be found by themselves in some levels and are sometimes locked in chests. Look for a key somewhere in the level, pick it up, and then carry it to the chest. Keys open chests and inside you find blue stars.

> There is one blue star in each level when you are playing a single-player game. Therefore, you can completely upgrade a costume in each level you play.

> In multiplayer games, there are fewer stars than there are players in each level. Therefore, it is a competition to get as many as you can. While the other players are fighting enemies or working on objectives, go after the blue stars.

WORLD COLLECTIBLES

Each world has its own unique collectible. There are three collectibles in each level, for a total of nine collectibles in each location and 27 in each world. Get all three collectibles within a level and you can unlock music, concept art, or character models for the current world.

World Collectibles

Aladdin	Alice
Lion King	Monsters, Inc.
Pirates of the Caribbean	WALL-E

AWARDS AND GRADES

At the end of each location, each of which includes three levels, all of the players are rated based on their performance. If you are playing by yourself, you still receive a grade. Based on your rating you can receive one of four different awards: gold, silver, bronze, or loser. Ratings take several factors into account: enemies defeated, gold collected, stars collected, and gold challenge medals won. The ratings are based on percentages. Here is what you need to do to earn three of the ratings:

100% - Silver	99-50% - Bronze	49-0% - Loser

Let's take a look at what you need to get the Silver grade.

- **GOLD:** Gold makes up 40% of your total. Collect 1,600 gold over the course of the three levels in a location to get 40% towards your grade. Get another 200 gold to increase this to 45%.

- **ENEMIES DEFEATED:** Defeat 70 enemies to get another 30% of your total. Defeat an extra 15 enemies during the three levels of a location to increase your percentage.

- **GOLD CHALLENGE MEDALS:** Earn a gold challenge medal in each of the three arcade challenges for 15%. (Each is worth 5%).

- **COLLECT BLUE STARS:** This is for another 15%. If you are playing with one or two players, you need to collect 3 stars. For 3 players you need 6 stars and then 9 stars if you have four players.

Note that these totals are cumulative for all players. Therefore, when playing with other players, you do not have to get 1,600 gold all by yourself. Instead, all players must collect a total of 1,600 gold to get the 40%. If you miss out on some of the arcade challenges or blue stars, be sure to collect 200 extra gold or defeat 15 more enemies to help make up for this.

The gold grade is tougher to earn. In fact, you must play through a location twice to even be eligible to earn it. To get the gold grade, you first have to meet the requirements for the silver grade. Then you also have to do the following:

- **WORLD COLLECTIBLES:** Collect all nine (three in each level) collectibles in the world.

- **GUESTS:** Free both guests. You can only free one guest on your first time playing through a location and must then play the location again to rescue the second guest.

During a game with other players, it is easy to see which player is currently in the lead. There is a star in the circle around their base.

The player with the star is the target for the other players. Help that player respawn by attacking him or her. Decrease the leader's grade so you can improve yours.

In addition to receiving a grade for each location, you also are graded for worlds. This grade take the average of all three locations within the world, so you have to earn gold grades in all three locations to get a gold grade for a world.

WORLD BEATER
Get a gold grade for a world and you receive this award.

CHAMPION OF THE UNIVERSE
Get a gold grade for all worlds to earn this award.

MULTIPLAYER

Playing *Disney Universe* on your own is a lot of fun as you take on HEX and his minions single-handedly. However, playing with other players adds a new dimension to the game, as you work together while also competing against each other at the same time.

Playing As a Team

When you play through the worlds with another player, you go through the same levels, fight against the same enemies, and complete the same objectives. However, during multiplayer games, you are not alone. You have one or more players to help you out. While you can all share the responsibilities of getting through a level, it is a good idea to focus on each player's strengths. Those players who have mastered the fighting combos and know how to defeat the mini-bosses can be in charge of fighting enemies. Some players may be good at jumping across gaps or up to high platforms. They should be the ones to go after items you need to complete the objectives. Divide up the tasks and you can get through the levels quickly and without having a lot of respawns.

Since in a *Disney Universe* game you are all playing on the same console and in the same room, talk to each other! Communication is the key to success. If you see a mini-boss appear, let the other players know in case they are concentrating on an objective. Sometimes six or eight eyes is better than only two.

ALONG FOR THE RIDE
Complete a level in multiplayer to earn this award.

ALL TOGETHER NOW
Complete a level with four players and you can earn this award as well.

Playing Against Each Other

While you can play cooperatively with other players, you are also competing against each other for grades and awards. Therefore, don't forget that to win, you have to beat the other players. Learn what it takes in improve your grade and what will lower the grade of the other players. Coins and collectibles are big helps to your grade. Also, keep your respawns low. To lower the grade of other players, attack them, pick them up and throw them, or "accidently" hit them with ground slam attacks or while using power-ups to defeat enemies. Of course, since they are right there in the room with you, don't forget some good-natured trash talk. Keep it nice and clean, but let them know you are there and are going to be the one to go home with the gold grade.

While you may want to directly attack other players, you must balance this with completing the levels and defeating the enemies. If you are constantly attacking other players, they will either gang up on you or not want to play with you. Therefore, be sly so they don't realize what hit them, or just use attacks that cause area damage when fighting enemies near the other players.

TO INFINITY . . . AND BEYOND!
Defeat another player by throwing them to earn this reward.

PLAYING TO WIN!
Earn this award by defeating five players in a single level.

COSTUME SHOP

Disney Universe has 45 different costumes available. You begin the game having access to nine of the costumes and unlock the 36 other costumes by rescuing guests to complete the locations in the various worlds. Be sure to get them all by unlocking them first, then purchasing them in the Costumes menu!

To free all the guests and unlock all the costumes, you must play through all locations twice.

The second time you play a location will be a lot harder than the first. I will make sure of it.

TOOLS

Each costume comes with its own unique tool which you can use to hit enemies and objects. As you are playing through the various levels, look for blue stars. They can be out in the open or locked up in chests. Find keys to unlock the chest and get the blue stars to upgrade your tool to the next level.

As your tool is upgraded by collecting blue stars, it gains extra powers which are released by ground slam attacks. At level 2, your tool releases an electrical charge that shocks nearby enemies. While they are stunned you can easily defeat them with another hit or two.

Upgrade to level 3 and your tool now has a fire attack, causing more damage to the area of the slam attack as well as firing off small fireballs that damage whatever they hit—including you. Be ready to jump up into the air to avoid those fireballs.

Finally, upgrade again to level 4 and your tool has a magical attack that damages enemies in a larger radius. Try to fully upgrade the tools for each of your costumes. All you have to do is collect three blue stars which can be accomplished while you play through the three levels in each location.

FOUR STAR COSTUME!
Fully upgrade a costume to earn this award

DRESSED FOR SUCCESS!
Unlock all of the costumes and then purchase all of them to receive this well-earned reward.

WORLD OF HURT!
Fully upgrade all five of a world's costumes and you get this award.

ULTIMATE COSMIC POWER!
If you can fully upgrade all of the costumes in the game, you definitely deserve this award.

ANGELICA

How to unlock:
Unlocked at the start.

Level 1	Level 2	Level 3	Level 4

BARBOSSA

How to unlock:
Complete *Alice* Wonderland Woods.

Level 1	Level 2	Level 3	Level 4

GIBBS

How to unlock:
Complete *Aladdin* Cave of Wonders two times.

Level 1	Level 2	Level 3	Level 4

JACK SPARROW

How to unlock:
Complete *Pirates of the Caribbean* Fountain of Youth.

Level 1	Level 2	Level 3	Level 4

BLACKBEARD

How to unlock:
Complete *Pirates of the Caribbean* Fountain of Youth two times.

Level 1	Level 2	Level 3	Level 4

Alice

CHESHIRE CAT

How to unlock:
Unlocked at the start.

Level 1	Level 2	Level 3	Level 4

WHITE RABBIT

How to unlock:
Complete *Lion King* Lower Pride Rock.

Level 1	Level 2	Level 3	Level 4

RED QUEEN

How to unlock:
Complete *Pirates of the Caribbean* London two times.

Level 1	Level 2	Level 3	Level 4

MAD HATTER

How to unlock:
Complete *Alice* Inside the Red Castle two times.

Level 1	Level 2	Level 3	Level 4

ALICE

How to unlock:
Complete *Alice* Inside the Red Castle.

Level 1	Level 2	Level 3	Level 4

Lion King

PUMBA

How to unlock:
Unlocked at the start.

Level 1	Level 2	Level 3	Level 4

RAFIKI

How to unlock:
Complete *Alice* Wonderland Woods two times.

Level 1	Level 2	Level 3	Level 4

TIMON

How to unlock:
Complete *Monsters, Inc.* Monster Training.

Level 1	Level 2	Level 3	Level 4

SIMBA

How to unlock:
Complete *Lion King* Upper Pride Rock.

Level 1	Level 2	Level 3	Level 4

SCAR

How to unlock:
Complete *Lion King* Upper Pride Rock two times.

Level 1	Level 2	Level 3	Level 4

Monsters, Inc.

RANDALL

How to unlock:
Unlocked at the start.

Level 1	Level 2	Level 3	Level 4

CELIA

How to unlock:
Complete *WALL-E* Abandoned Earth.

Level 1	Level 2	Level 3	Level 4

SUSHI CHEF

How to unlock:
Complete *Lion King* Lower Pride Rock two times.

Level 1	Level 2	Level 3	Level 4

SULLY

How to unlock:
Complete *Monsters, Inc.* Door Factory two times.

Level 1	Level 2	Level 3	Level 4

MIKE

How to unlock:
Complete *Monsters, Inc.* Door Factory.

Level 1	Level 2	Level 3	Level 4

Aladdin

JASMINE

How to unlock:
Unlocked at the start.

Level 1	Level 2	Level 3	Level 4

ABU

How to unlock:
Complete *WALL-E* Abandoned Earth two times.

Level 1	Level 2	Level 3	Level 4

IAGO

How to unlock:
Complete *Pirates of the Caribbean* London.

Level 1	Level 2	Level 3	Level 4

ALADDIN

How to unlock:
Complete *Aladdin* Agrabah Palace.

Level 1	Level 2	Level 3	Level 4

JAFAR

How to unlock:
Complete *Aladdin* Agrabah Palace two times.

Level 1	Level 2	Level 3	Level 4

Prima Official Game Guide

WALL-E

HAL

How to unlock:
Unlocked at the start.

Level 1	Level 2	Level 3	Level 4

BURN-E

How to unlock:
Complete *Monsters, Inc.*
Monster Training two times.

Level 1	Level 2	Level 3	Level 4

M-O

How to unlock:
Complete *Aladdin* Cave
of Wonders.

Level 1	Level 2	Level 3	Level 4

EVE

How to unlock:
Complete *WALL-E* Axiom
Captain's Deck two times.

Level 1	Level 2	Level 3	Level 4

WALL-E

How to unlock:
Complete *WALL-E* Axiom
Captain's Deck.

Level 1	Level 2	Level 3	Level 4

Disney 1

TRON

How to unlock:
Unlocked at the start.

Level 1	Level 2	Level 3	Level 4

CLU 2

How to unlock:
Complete *Alice* Over the Castle Wall two times.

Level 1	Level 2	Level 3	Level 4

QUORRA

How to unlock:
Complete *Pirates of the Caribbean Queen Anne's Revenge.*

Level 1	Level 2	Level 3	Level 4

SAM

How to unlock:
Complete *Aladdin* Streets of Agrabah.

Level 1	Level 2	Level 3	Level 4

STITCH

How to unlock:
Complete *Monsters. Inc.* High in the Himalayas.

Level 1	Level 2	Level 3	Level 4

Disney 2

MICKEY

How to unlock:
Unlocked at the start.

Level 1	Level 2	Level 3	Level 4

MINNIE

How to unlock:
Complete *Pirates of the Caribbean Queen Anne's Revenge* two times.

Level 1	Level 2	Level 3	Level 4

ARIEL

How to unlock:
Complete *Monsters. Inc. High in the Himalayas* two times.

Level 1	Level 2	Level 3	Level 4

NEMO

How to unlock:
Complete *Lion King Elephant Graveyard*.

Level 1	Level 2	Level 3	Level 4

BALOO

How to unlock:
Complete *Lion King Elephant Graveyard* two times.

Level 1	Level 2	Level 3	Level 4

Disney 3

DONALD

How to unlock:
Unlocked at the start.

Level 1 | Level 2 | Level 3 | Level 4

GOOFY

How to unlock:
Complete *Alice* Over the Castle Wall.

Level 1 | Level 2 | Level 3 | Level 4

ROBIN HOOD

How to unlock:
Complete *WALL-E Axiom* Belowdecks two times.

Level 1 | Level 2 | Level 3 | Level 4

RAPUNZEL

How to unlock:
Complete *Aladdin* Streets of Agrabah two times.

Level 1 | Level 2 | Level 3 | Level 4

TINKERBELL

How to unlock:
Complete *WALL-E Axiom* Belowdecks.

Level 1 | Level 2 | Level 3 | Level 4

HEX'S BOTS

HEX does not want you to rescue the guests trapped in the Disney Universe. Therefore, HEX has taken control of all the bots and turned them against you and all the other guests. While the bots were originally designed to be harmless, they now attack you on sight. All of the bots in *Disney Universe* are dressed in costumes to fit in with the various worlds. Therefore, the bots in the *Pirates of the Caribbean* world are dressed as British soldiers in their redcoat uniforms or as parrots, while the bots in the *Lion King* world are disguised as animals.

As you damage bots, they begin to lose their costumes. When you see this occur, you know you need to get in only another hit or two to finish them off.

FODDER

Fodder are the basic bots and the main soldiers in HEX's army. They come in two different varieties and attack you at all times and in all places.

Standard Fodder

The most common bot in the *Disney Universe*, the standard Fodder is humanoid in appearance with two arms and two legs. Fodder can attack with their hands, though they are often armed with a tool similar to that carried by characters of their particular world. Some Fodder can carry ranged weapons such as ray guns or rifles, which allow them to attack you from a distance.

In addition to attacking, Fodder also like to move important items. Don't be surprise if they walk off with a key or move objects you need away from you or out of position. Some Fodder construct traps or activate levers and switches—especially when these can hurt you. Fodder can ride animals and they will use the animals to attack you.

Fodder often attack you in groups rather than one at a time. They are much more dangerous in groups. Use simple attacks chained together so that you get a finishing move when attacking them. The ground slam attack or uppercut slam both work well because these combos have an area effect and damage all enemies near the point of impact.

Watch out for Fodder with guns. They can stay back out of range of your tool and cause damage to you. Sometimes they are off screen, so if you start taking damage for no apparent reason, look for a Fodder with a gun.

Flying Fodder

Flying Fodder are essentially Fodder with wings. These are actually one of the tougher types of Fodder since they not only fly around, but can also fire at you green projectiles that cause damage. Flying Fodder also fly high enough that they can avoid your simple attacks. Instead of using these, face them and perform a jump attack so you can get high enough to hit them. Once hit by your tool, a Flying Fodder drops to the ground and is stunned for a few seconds. Quickly move in and finish it off before it recovers and takes off again.

Before a Flying Fodder fires at you, it gets a greenish glow as it powers up for the shot. Attack it as soon as you see it power up to defeat it and prevent the shot, or else be ready to dodge out of the way of the projectile.

MINI-BOSSES

HEX has some larger bots to take you on as well. These mini-bosses are stronger, can cause more damage, and take more hits before they are defeated. Each type also has special attacks they use to try to make you respawn.

Do you really think I am going to give you any tips on how to defeat my bots? Just give up now while you still can. I will win!

Brute

The Brute is the basic mini-boss. It is like a big standard Fodder with two arms and two legs. Brutes have several different attacks. If you are close to one, it will try to grab you and then punch you while in its grip. If this happens, press the Use button rapidly to break away. Brutes also charge at you if they are at a distance and then jump up and slam down into the ground. This causes damage to anyone near the impact. After this attack, the Brute gets stuck into the ground for a short time, which gives you a great chance to move in for an attack while it can't fight back. Finally, the Brute punches down into the ground for a slam attack. Again, it gets stuck, so move in and attack before it can recover.

When facing a Brute, try to use ground slam attacks to cause extra damage. While you can attack it at all times, it is best to wait until it is stuck after it performs one of its attacks. Quickly get in a few hits and then get back.

When a Brute is making a charge attack, a button icon appears on the screen. Press that button to sidestep and dodge the attack. This leaves the Brute stunned and stuck, so go in for the attack.

THE BIGGER THEY ARE . . .
. . . the harder they fall. Defeat your first Brute to earn this award.

Roto

The Roto is the next mini-boss you must face off against. It has one regular arm and one arm with a wrecking ball on the end. The Roto has three different attacks. The Roto can thrust the ball at you in a long-range punch attack. Therefore, if it is not moving around, stay back and avoid getting hit. During the second type of attack, the Roto moves around as it spins its ball low in a circle. Don't try to attack the bot during this low spin attack since the Roto can't be damaged. The Roto can also spin the ball up high in a larger circle while remaining in one spot.

You can damage the Roto during its high spin attack, but be careful because you are likely to take some

hits as well. Instead, wait until after the Roto finishes a high spin attack and becomes dizzy. Then move in and attack it while it can't hit you back. When the mini-boss starts spinning again, get out of the way and wait for another opportunity to get in some hits. Rotos are easier to fight when you have lots of room to move around. However, in small areas, try to jump up onto higher platforms to avoid the attacks or just keep moving around and don't get caught in a corner from which you can't escape.

DIZZY!
Defeat a Roto for the first time to earn this award.

Bulldog

The Bulldog is a mini-boss that is typically assigned to guard a location—one that players need to get to. Bulldogs charge any players who get close to their area. As you are being charged, watch for a button icon to appear and quickly press that button to avoid the charge and put yourself in a position to counter-attack the Bulldog. After a Bulldog completes its charge, it acts stunned for a bit. In addition to charging, the Bulldog can also grab players who are close to it and shake them with its mouth to cause damage.

The keys to defeating a Bulldog are to avoid its charges and, when it is recovering from a charge, to move in to hit it with slam attacks. Quickly get back so that the Bulldog can't grab and shake you.

BAD DOG!
Defeat your first Bulldog to earn this award.

Spawner

The Spawner is the fourth mini-boss. It gets its name from its ability to send Fodder to attack you. It can also fire large fireballs. Fight off the Fodder that the Spawner sends your way and then get in close for an attack. The Spawner also attacks by sitting on you or bumping into you to knock you off a platform.

When you see the Spawner's cannon charging up and getting ready to fire, be ready to press the Use button as the fireball gets close to you. This hits the fireball back at the Spawner and stuns it so you can move in and attack without worrying about getting hurt.

 It is usually a good idea to save VIC cubes for fighting against mini-bosses. Those power-ups that cause single-hit defeats can cause a lot of damage against mini-bosses and some are so powerful that a few hits will do the job.

TIME FOR A DIET!
Defeat your first Spawner in order to receive this award.

TRAPS

In some areas, Fodder set up safety cones and begin constructing traps. During the construction, these Fodder do not attack and are vulnerable to your attacks. Traps can be destroyed by hitting them with ground slam attacks. Some traps can take more damage, so you will have to use more than one attack to destroy them.

 The best time to destroy a trap is while it is still being built by a Fodder. Attack the Fodder and force it to fight against you. If a Fodder does not continue constructing the trap, it disappears.

Don't think you are safe just because you destroy a trap. I will send more Fodder to rebuild it. So watch your back.

Spike Trap

Spike traps are pretty common traps. Fodder like to build them in front of switches or doorways to stop you from getting where you need to go. If you touch a spike trap, you lose all your health and respawn. Therefore, be careful around these traps. A ground slam attack next to a spike trap destroys it so you can then move across the ground without getting hurt.

> It is a good idea to destroy spike traps whenever you see them, even though you may not think they are in your way. If a mini-boss appears and you need to move out of the way quickly, the spike traps could be deadly.

Cannon Trap

While not actually a trap, Fodder like to build these in the middle of areas. Consisting of a cannon set on a tall turret, cannon traps fire cannon balls at you that cause a lot of damage if they hit you. Destroy cannon traps as quickly as possible. They often can fire only in certain directions, so try to get in behind the cannons and ground slam attack them. These take several attacks to destroy. Cannon traps can fire from off-screen, so if you start getting hit by explosions, look for the cannon trap and move in close to destroy it.

> Bombs work great for destroying all types of traps. If you can find a pile of them, pick up a bomb and throw it at a trap. It may take a couple of explosions to destroy the trap, but you can get rid of them without having to get in close.

Barrier

The last kind of trap is the barrier. Fodder like to build these in front of doorways or exits to prevent you from getting to items or moving to new areas. These often take several hits by ground slam attacks before they are destroyed. If you have a cannon, drive one over and fire at a barrier to get it out of your way.

SECRETS AND AWARDS

Disney Universe is filled with collectibles and awards. This chapter shows you where to find all the collectibles for each of the six worlds as well as how to earn the achievements.

WORLD COLLECTIBLES

Each world contains 27 collectibles unique to that world. There are three collectibles in each level and once you find all three in a level, you unlock either music, concept art, or character models for that world.

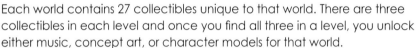

Pirates of the Caribbean—Ships in a Bottle

LONDON LEVEL 1

Shoot the door with the target on it by the bridge to blast it open. Inside you can get the first ship in a bottle.

As you perform the double-jump to get across the gap on the bridge, be sure to pick up the second ship in a bottle along the way. If you miss it, perform a double-jump back to the left and try again.

The third ship in a bottle is located to the right of the stairs at the far-right side of this area.

LONDON LEVEL 2

The first ship in a bottle is to the right of the cargo nets.

Walk up the steps to the right and get the ship in a bottle that is under a cargo net.

You can find the third ship in a bottle below the spinning wheel. Be sure to pick it up before exiting the level.

LONDON LEVEL 3

The first ship in a bottle is near the building right at the start.

A second ship in a bottle is near the cannon on the area's left side.

The third ship in a bottle is in the bottom-right corner of this area.

QUEEN ANNE'S REVENGE LEVEL 1

Carry Triton's sword to a socket next to a skeleton on the far-left side of the foredeck where you begin. Once you insert the sword into the socket, a plank extends from the deck, which allows you to walk along it to get the first ship in a bottle.

Place the sword into the socket by the side of the ship next to a skeleton; another plank extends from the ship. Walk out onto it to get the second ship in a bottle.

Once you get to the right side, break up some crates near the side of the ship so that you can collect the third ship in a bottle.

QUEEN ANNE'S REVENGE LEVEL 2

Place the sword in the socket by the skeleton, then walk out onto the plank to get the first ship in a bottle for this level.

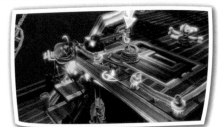

Move to the small platform by the socket with the sword in it and stand on the footprints. As the cage swings over you, press the Use button to grab onto it and swing across to get the second ship in a bottle.

Jump over the railing on the upper deck and land on a canopy to find the third ship in a bottle.

QUEEN ANNE'S REVENGE LEVEL 3

Pull the green lever next to the wheel's cell to open another cell, where you can pick up a ship in a bottle.

Place the green lever in the switch on the right side and pull on it to open a cell holding the second ship in a bottle.

Climb back up onto the right walkway and stand on the footprint pad. Grab on to the cage as it swings by and ride it out over the main floor to get the final ship in a bottle.

FOUNTAIN OF YOUTH LEVEL 1

After fighting the enemies on the shore, jump up onto the ledge at the rear of the area, then head to the left. Jump across to a rocky platform to get the first ship in a bottle in this level.

After going down in to the water as a zombie and pulling the lever, move to the left and cut down some coral so you can get to another alcove with a ship in a bottle inside.

Drive the cannon to the right side of this area and fire at the targets on door across the water. One of the doors has a ship in a bottle behind it.

FOUNTAIN OF YOUTH LEVEL 2

Walk along the bottom of the sea as a zombie toward the left. Attack the coral and ride wooden platforms to the surface to get the first ship in a bottle.

Jump across the second set of barrels to collect the second ship in a bottle, which floats up in the air between them.

Pull the green lever to retracts some spears. Now hop onto a duck and sail it over to the right to collect the third ship in a bottle where the spears used to be guarding it.

FOUNTAIN OF YOUTH LEVEL 3

Pick up bombs and throw them at the targets on the wooden doors to blow them open. A door underneath the cannon on the left has a ship in a bottle behind it. So, once the door is splinters, get the bottle.

Change into a zombie and go into the water. Cut away the coral behind the spears so you can get to the second ship in a bottle hidden underneath the statue of a head.

Pick up a bomb and quickly run up the ramp along the right side of the area. Throw the bomb at the door next to the red switch. After the door is gone, collect the third ship in a bottle.

Alice—Drink Me Bottles

WONDERLAND WOODS LEVEL 1

Before leaving this first area, step on this red switch, which makes a rock ledge extend from the rock wall. Then head up the stairs and go through the door to get to the platform where you found the first chess piece. From there, jump across to the ledge and then jump again to get the drink me bottle.

While you are getting the chess piece on the back left platform, jump across to a couple of ledges to get a second drink me bottle.

Before you exit the level, carry a pocket watch up the stairs and place it into the socket on the right side. This opens an alcove where you can get the third drink me bottle.

WONDERLAND WOODS LEVEL 2

Go through the door on the upper ledge. It takes you to a mushroom where you can get the first drink me bottle.

Carry the pocket watch toward the front of the level and insert it into a socket to remove some vines and get the second drink me bottle.

Move the spoon catapult by pushing it so that it is targeting the stack of cups by the hat. Jump up onto the handle of the spoon to launch a sugar cube at the cups. Launch more sugar cubes until the cups are all broken and a drink me bottle is revealed. Then jump into the hat and fire yourself up to get the bottle

WONDERLAND WOODS LEVEL 3

Place the pocket watch in the socket near at the bottom of the stairs to open an alcove and get the drink me bottle hidden inside.

Go back and pick up the pocket watch and then place it in the socket under the tree limb on the right side to raise up a container. Climb up the stairs and jump from the ledge across to the container and then onto the limb to get the second drink me bottle.

Pull on the present to the right of the cake roll to open it and get the third drink me bottle and unlock some character models.

OVER THE CASTLE WALL 1

The first drink me bottle is floating above the river. You must use the hat to get to it. As the floating hat moves toward the bottle, step on the red switch on the right side of the river to close the mouths of the heads and then jump into the hat. You drop down from the other hat, collecting the bottle as you fall. You have to be quick to jump from the boat on which you land since it will be heading over the waterfall.

Jump into the hat and shoot yourself up into the blue hat when the other floating blue hat is underneath the drink me bottle.

Jump into the hat and watch the rotating hat. As it rotates and is pointing toward the left, shoot yourself into the other purple hat so you warp out and fly up into the air to get the third drink me bottle.

OVER THE CASTLE WALL LEVEL 2

Use the hat to get to the top of the platform with two cages on it. Move one of the cages to find a drink me bottle behind it.

Pull on the green lever to extend a walkway across the pit. Then step on the red switch on the left. This lifts the cage on the left and extends two small platforms. Move down the walkway and then jump across to the platform to get the second drink me bottle.

Step on the switch inside the cell to make the platforms extend again if necessary and jump up out of the pit. Go back around and do the same thing again—this time stepping on the right red switch—and then go get the third drink me bottle.

OVER THE CASTLE WALL LEVEL 3

After you place the first three cards on the table, the Red Queen drops a drink me bottle near the table, so pick it up and add it to your collection.

Move the hat onto the pad and use it to get up to the higher platform where the second drink me bottle is located.

Move the hat to the pad on the right side to get to the third drink me bottle.

INSIDE THE RED CASTLE LEVEL 1

Near where you began the level, jump across to a floating card and ride it around through the air to get the first drink me bottle. Then, as the card returns near the wall, jump back onto the castle.

Jump into the hat and warp to an enclosed section of the maze. Watch out for the arrows in the sidewalk and, when it is clear, grab the drink me bottle in the middle.

The third drink me bottle is located next to the spade.

INSIDE THE RED CASTLE LEVEL 2

Hit the high grass along the left side of the area to cut it down. Not only do you find coins there, but also the first drink me bottle.

Take control of the catapult on the right. Aim it at the target by the Red Queen sign on the right. When you hit the target, a drink me bottle drops down. Pick it up.

Before going through the exit, launch the ball one more time. Do the same thing you did for the spade by using the steam switches and the heart platform on the left. When the ball reaches the end, the drink me bottle inside is released for you to pick up.

INSIDE THE RED CASTLE LEVEL 3

After you destroy one of the Jabber-wocky's hands, a drink me bottle appears. Fight your way through the enemies to get to it.

As soon as you destroy the second hand, pick up another drink me bottle.

As the Jabberwocky falls from the walls of the castle, it leaves behind the last drink me bottle.

Lion King—Grubs

LOWER PRIDE ROCK LEVEL 1

While you are up by the piles of bombs, throw a bomb at the rock near the key. Once it is gravel, jump up and get your first grub.

A red switch is under the tree you can knock down with a bomb. Step on this switch to open a cage to the left. Inside, get the second grub. Yummmm!

Step on the red switch near the pile of bombs; a ledge will extend out from the cliff side. Drop down to the ledge to get the third grub.

LOWER PRIDE ROCK LEVEL 2

Step on the red switch near the pile of bombs and then drop down to the ledge to get your first grub of the level.

A second grub is behind the two rocks to the right of the key. Use another bomb to blow up the rocks and then get the grub.

Pick up a seed from the tree and plant it near the rocky platform where you can see a grub. Water the seed and, after it grows, jump up on the leaves to get the third grub.

LOWER PRIDE ROCK LEVEL 3

Pick up a bomb and throw it at the rock next to the crank. After it blows up, pick up the grub that was hiding behind the rock.

Throw a water balloon at the flames on the far right of the area so you can get the second grub.

Use the cannon to shoot at the rock on top of the middle platform. After destroying it, jump up onto the platform to get the third grub.

ELEPHANT GRAVEYARD LEVEL 1

On the same platform as the key, be sure to pick up the first grub.

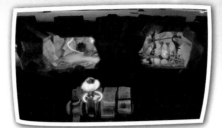

Before leaving the first area, move to the near-right corner and drop down onto a walkway. Step on a red switch to start a platform moving back and forth. Jump onto the platform and ride it past some cages. Use slam attacks to break open the cages. Inside of one is a grub.

Step on the red switch near the front of this area. Then drop down onto some ledges that extend from the cliff side. Collect the third grub.

ELEPHANT GRAVEYARD LEVEL 2

Start off the level by getting your first grub. Throw a water balloon at the seed in the far-left corner. Then jump up onto the leaves of the plant so that you can get to the grub.

Step on the red switch next to the cannon, then jump down to a couple of ledges to get the second grub.

Jump up the stone steps to get to the top. However, before you go through the exit, jump over to a platform to the left and get the third grub.

ELEPHANT GRAVEYARD LEVEL 3

Step on the red switch near where you start, then jump down to a ledge where you can find the first grub.

While next to the third organ key on the ledge, pick up a water balloon and jump up to a higher ledge to water a seed. After a tree grows, a grub appears. Jump up onto the tree to collect it.

Use the cannon to shoot at the target at the area's far-left edge. This causes a ledge with a grub to drop down. Move to the ledge and collect the third grub.

UPPER PRIDE ROCK LEVEL 1

Stop at the dock on the far-left side of the area and get off. Jump up onto the top of the ledge and collect the first grub. Then sail the duck over to the island.

While you are on the duck, be sure to hit the target on the lake's far-right side. You have to fire across the island to hit it. When it's hit, the target flips over a rock, creating a platform in the lava. Now you can jump from the island to a ledge on the side of the lake of lava using this platform and get a second grub.

Go back to the cannon and fire at the target near the lava flow. As the lava adds weight on one end of this crane, the other rises, bringing a grub up with it.

UPPER PRIDE ROCK LEVEL 2

Pick up a bomb and throw it at the rock with the target on it. After it blows up, get the grub that was hiding on the other side.

Turn the crank on the left so that the flow goes down to a small stone platform. Pull the green lever to send lava into the channel and then jump onto the platform. The lava raises it up so you can jump up and get the second grub.

Pick up a water balloon and throw it at the seed by the lever. When the tree grows, jump up onto its leaves to get the third grub.

UPPER PRIDE ROCK LEVEL 3

Pick up a water balloon and throw it at the seed on the front-left corner. Then jump up onto the tree to get a grub.

Do the same in the front-right corner so you can also get the second grub. Be sure to get these before leaving this area. There is no coming back.

Move the drum on the left side of the area to the back and place it under the grub. Then jump onto the drum and shoot yourself up to get the third grub and unlock character models.

Monsters. Inc.—Fuzzy Dice

MONSTER TRAINING LEVEL 1

Step on the red switch and a platform lowers. Jump up onto it to get the fuzzy dice.

Step on the red switch to lower a platform. Then jump up onto the platform to get the second pair of fuzzy dice.

Before going through the exit, walk to the left to find a door. Go through it into a room in the house. Pull the lever at the back of the room to reverse gravity so that you can get the fuzzy dice on the ceiling.

MONSTER TRAINING LEVEL 2

Walk up the stairs to the right and stand by the door. Wait until the door at the top moves next to the fuzzy dice, then go through the door to get the dice.

Step on the left arrow to make the lift go to the left. When you are as far as you can go, step on the back arrow to raise the lift. Jump off to the left to get the pair of fuzzy dice.

While you are getting the final door piece in the upper balcony, be sure to collect the third pair of fuzzy dice.

MONSTER TRAINING LEVEL 3

Step on the four red switches on the right side of the level to open a door. Inside is the first pair of fuzzy dice.

After the second set of doors leaves and enemies arrive, a pair of fuzzy dice is dropped off in the back-left area of the floor. Go pick them up and add them to your collection.

After completing the third set of doors, the third pair of fuzzy dice appears to the right of the canister slots.

HIGH IN THE HIMALAYAS LEVEL 1

With a lantern in hand, walk toward the front of the area and melt the ice surrounding the first pair of fuzzy dice.

Go back to where you picked up the first snow cone, then move to the right and jump out onto the ice flows in a river. Collect another pair of fuzzy dice floating in the air above the middle of the river.

After jumping up the stone blocks to get the first door piece, pick up a third pair of fuzzy dice while you are there.

HIGH IN THE HIMALAYAS LEVEL 2

The first pair of fuzzy dice is just to the left of the entrance. Carefully melt the ice blocks, leaving one on the right side so that you can use the ice block and stone blocks to jump up and get the dice.

More fuzzy dice are by the snowmobile. Carefully use the lantern to melt some of the ice blocks. Leave three on the left side. Jump up the blocks to get the dice.

Carefully drop down off the edge of the frozen river and land on a ledge where the third pair of fuzzy dice is hiding.

HIGH IN THE HIMALAYAS LEVEL 3

Move all the way to the far-right side of the level and get rid of the ice surrounding the first pair of fuzzy dice so you can pick them up.

The second pair of fuzzy dice is hiding behind the targets. After shooting the targets to make the bridge, walk to the edge of the frozen river and jump up to get the dice.

While on the ledge with the snow cone, jump across to the right and land in the damaged roof of the nearby shack to get the third pair of fuzzy dice.

DOOR FACTORY LEVEL 1

At the top of the stairs, go through the door next to the wall. This takes you up onto a narrow walkway. Go to the end to get a pair of fuzzy dice.

Step on the red switch to halt the doors here so that you can walk out onto a platform and get a second pair of fuzzy dice.

Place the keycard in the reader to open the door. Pick up the third pair of fuzzy dice.

DOOR FACTORY LEVEL 2

Blow up every single door so that none remain. A pair of fuzzy dice appears for you to collect.

Press the red switch on the right side to slow down the conveyor belt of doors for a short time. Quickly move across the doors, picking up a second pair of fuzzy dice along the way.

Blow up all the red doors by the exit to make a third pair of fuzzy dice appear.

DOOR FACTORY LEVEL 3

Jump across to the right conveyor belt to get the pair of fuzzy dice.

As you are racing, jump over to the right conveyor belt. Then, as the doors are coming at you, jump over to a platform on the right to get the fuzzy dice.

Jump on the pad on the right side to bounce up to get the third pair of fuzzy dice.

Aladdin—Gems

CAVE OF WONDERS LEVEL 1

Move the lantern down the platform and toward the place where you entered the Cave of Wonders. The lantern causes bridge sections to appear so that you can move across to the first gem.

Take the lantern to the front of the area between the two platforms where you found the scarab pieces. There, you can find the second gem.

Move the lantern to the far-left side of the upper area to reveal the third gem.

CAVE OF WONDERS LEVEL 2

Take the lantern to the front of the upper area to reveal a red switch. Step on it to make the monkey statue below, where you already returned a ruby, rise up to reveal a gem. Jump back down the stone steps to get the gem.

Move the lantern farther to the right and across more bridge sections to find the second gem.

Move a lantern to the area to the left of the monkey statue to find the third gem.

CAVE OF WONDERS LEVEL 3

Jump across a series of stone steps to get to the first gem. These steps collapse soon after you step on them, so be quick and accurate. You get only one chance to get this gem.

Place the scarab piece in the statue to release a flying scarab. Jump over the trap and follow the scarab as it reveals bridge sections that lead to the second gem.

Take the ruby to the monkey statue and place it in the statue's hands. Some stone steps appear to the right. Jump up them to get the third gem.

STREETS OF AGRABAH LEVEL 1

At the start, pick up a bomb and throw it at the dome to the right to find the first gem.

Go back to the first area near where the key was located. Look at the colors of the notes above a door. Go back to the organ and play those notes in the same order by jumping onto those keys. This opens the door so that you can get the gem inside.

Move the lamp to the round pad by the well to create a geyser that carries you up to get the third gem.

STREETS OF AGRABAH LEVEL 2

Go back to the fire-eater and drag him up the steps to the next area. Place him on the red pad so he burns a cage and reveals the first gem.

Take the snake charmer to the green pad on the right and then climb up the rope to get to the second gem.

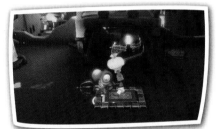

To get the third gem, drag the sword swallower down to the first area and place him on the blue pad in front of building where the lamp was. This opens the sword barrier for you.

STREETS OF AGRABAH LEVEL 3

Drop back down to the street and place the lamp on the pad near the well. Ride the geyser up to get to the balcony, where you can find some coins and a gem.

Take the sword swallower all the way to the left side of the level and place him on the blue pad to clear the sword barrier so that you can get the second gem.

Take the lamp to the pad by the musical instrument booth and change it into a giant pipe organ. Play the colored notes that can be found above the door on the level's far-right side to open the door. Get the gem inside.

AGRABAH PALACE LEVEL 1

Walk to the front and then along the walkway to the left. Jump onto the cushion to bounce up and get the first gem.

Drag the fire-eater into the small room to the left and put him on the red pad. After he lights the bowl held by the elephant statue, a gem appears for you to collect.

Place the sword swallower on the blue pad in the room on the left to remove the sword barrier. Then drag the fire-eater onto the red pad to make the third gem appear.

AGRABAH PALACE LEVEL 2

Look in a little alcove on the room's left side to find the first gem.

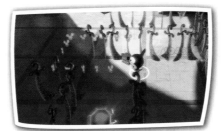

A gem is waiting in the middle of the maze. Work your way around to get to it. Or you can just uncover all the pictures and pick it up at the end.

Before you exit, drag the fire-eater into the room with the spears and the handle. Place him on the red pad to light the bowl and make the third gem appear.

AGRABAH PALACE LEVEL 3

This level is a boss battle and it takes place in the same area. At the start, rush over to the left side of the area and jump onto the cushion to bounce up and get the first gem.

While Jafar is transforming into a giant cobra, rush to the right side and bounce up from a cushion to get a second gem.

The final Gem can be found out in the open, near the top right corner of the battle area. Examine the circular platform near the top right, where Jafar pops out and you'll find the Gem ready to be claimed. Just be sure to grab it while Jafar is not attacking.

WALL-E—Combo Meals

ABANDONED EARTH LEVEL 1

Pick up one of the bombs that comes out of the pipes and throw it at the red trash blocks on the right side. When they blow up, a cage with a combo meal drops down. Throw another bomb at it and then collect it.

Use the arrow switches to move the magnet to the right and then back to lift two platforms so that you can jump up and get your second combo meal.

Jump onto the bouncy barrels to get over to the far-right area. Throw bombs at the red trash blocks to get the third combo meal at the back.

ABANDONED EARTH LEVEL 2

Before leaving the starting, low area, move into the open sewer tunnel. Go all the way to the back, turn left, and then come forward to get the first combo meal.

Jump to the left onto a couple of bouncy barrels to get the second combo meal.

Jump back up to the platform on the right. Step on the red switch, then stand on the arrow platform; it shoots you up to the top of some blocks, where you can get a third combo meal.

ABANDONED EARTH LEVEL 3

From the start, jump over to a bouncy barrel and then jump again to another barrel to get the first combo meal.

Pick up and throw bombs at the blocks on a lower level near the front of the area. Blow up the trash blocks and break open a cage to release a combo meal. Then jump across and pick it up.

Step on the red switch at the front of the final area to make three sewer doors open to form platforms. Drop through a gap on the left side of a chain-link barrier and jump across the platforms to get the combo meal. Then, quickly jump back across to the left before the time is up and the doors close.

AXIOM BELOWDECKS LEVEL 1

When you get a chance, step on the red switch at the front of the area to raise two platforms. Drop down and get the combo meal and some coins, then quickly jump back up to the main area before the timer runs out and the platforms move away.

Move a security bot over to a far-right position to activate a light track. Then stand on the footprint pad and press the Use button to climb up the light track to get onto a walkway. Step on the red switch and then jump down to get the combo meal before the door closes.

Stand on the footprint pad at the area's far-left corner and press the Use button to begin climbing it. Follow it along to the middle to get the combo meal.

AXIOM BELOWDECKS LEVEL 2

While you are on the ceiling, walk over to the left to pick up the first combo meal.

While on the ceiling in the second area, continue to the left side to get the second combo meal.

Drag the jump cannon from the right side over to the platform on the left. Jump into the cannon and then launch yourself up onto the platform to get the third combo meal.

AXIOM BELOWDECKS LEVEL 3

Step on the red switch in the front-left corner of the area to raise a couple of platforms. Then jump onto these platforms to get the first combo meal.

Move the jump cannon under the smasher and up the lift to the platform on the right. Use it to jump up to a smaller, higher platform, where you can get the second combo meal.

After the furnace is shut down, move inside it to collect the third combo meal.

AXIOM CAPTAIN'S DECK LEVEL 1

Drag the passenger over to the side and jump onto the passenger. You bounce up high. Land on the upper walkway and get a combo meal.

Move the passenger or the Captain over to the right side and jump on the bouncy person to get up to another walkway where the second combo meal can be found.

After getting back down to the main deck, move the passenger or Captain to the right and jump up to another higher area. Step on the red switch and then quickly stand on the round pad, which springs you up into the air to get the third combo meal.

AXIOM CAPTAIN'S DECK LEVEL 2

Scan the boot with the plant in it, then walk into the room with the power block and pick up the first combo meal.

Go back across the bridge and toward the back where the energy field was to get the second combo meal.

Step on the red switch near the front of the last area. Quickly walk onto the round pad and spring up to get the third combo meal.

AXIOM CAPTAIN'S DECK LEVEL 3

After attacking Auto, a combo meal appears to the right side. Pick it up and add it to your collection.

After hitting Auto and defeating it, another combo meal appears to the left.

After activating the consoles for the first time, this Combo Meal appears the top center of the room, between the two computer consoles. You can grab it as soon as it appears, but it's probably best to wait until the coast is clear to pick it up. You can even grab it once you've defeated Auto!

AWARDS

As you play through the game, you can earn achievements or trophies by completing worlds, collecting the world collectibles, purchasing and upgrading costumes, and defeating enemies. Try to get all of these.

Xbox 360 Achievements

Name	Description	Points
Saviour of the Universe!	Complete all of the worlds	90
Hero of the Sands	Complete the *Aladdin* world	15
Time for Tea!	Complete the *Alice* world	15
It means no worries!	Complete the *Lion King* world	15
Scary Feet!	Complete the *Monsters, Inc.* world	15
Swash Buckler	Complete the *Pirates of the Caribbean* world	15
Returning to Earth	Complete the *WALL-E* world	15
World Beater	Get a gold grade for a world	30
Champion of the Universe	Get a gold grade for all worlds	90
Collector	Collect all of the world collectables within one level	15
Serious Collector	Collect all of the world collectables within a location	15
World Set Complete!	Collect all of the world collectables within a world	30
Compulsive Collector	Collect all of the world collectables in the game	90
Suit Up!	Purchase a costume	15
Dressed for Success!	Purchase all of the costumes	30
Four Star Costume!	Fully upgrade a costume	15
World of Hurt!	Fully upgrade all of a world's costumes	30
Ultimate Cosmic Power!	Fully upgrade all of the costumes in the game	90
Challenge Addict	Play 50 challenges	15
For The Win!	Win 50 challenges	30
The bigger they are . . .	Defeat the Brute	15
Dizzy!	Defeat Roto	15
Time for a Diet!	Defeat the Spawner	15
Bad Dog!	Defeat the Bulldog	15
Gold Hoarder	Amass 1,000 coins in the bank	15
Richer than a McDuck!	Amass 10,000 coins in the bank	30
Along for the ride	Complete a level in multiplayer	15
All Together Now!	Complete a level with four players	15
Playing to win!	Defeat five players in a single level	15
To infinity . . . and beyond!	Defeat another player by throwing them	15
Keep 'em coming!	Defeat 100 enemies	15
Anti-Virus!	Defeat 500 enemies	30
Giddy Up!	Defeat an enemy whilst riding an animal	15
Freeze!	Defeat five enemies using a single Snowman power-up	15
Boxing Clever	Defeat five enemies using a single Power Punch power-up	15
Bad Hair Day	Defeat five enemies using a single Medusa power-up	15
Rapid Fire	Defeat five enemies using a single Shooter power-up	15
Tag! You're it!	Transfer a curse to another player	15
Unstoppable!	Complete a level without respawning	15
Old School	Complete a level without using help arrows	10

PlayStation 3 Trophies

Name	Description	Trophy
Saviour of the Universe!	Complete all of the worlds	Gold
Hero of the Sands	Complete the *Aladdin* world	Bronze
Time for Tea!	Complete the *Alice* world	Bronze
It means no worries!	Complete the *Lion King* world	Bronze
Scary Feet!	Complete the *Monsters, Inc.* world	Bronze
Swash Buckler	Complete the *Pirates of the Caribbean* world	Bronze
Returning to Earth	Complete the *WALL-E* world	Bronze
World Beater	Get a gold grade for a world	Silver
Champion of the Universe	Get a gold grade for all worlds	Gold
Collector	Collect all of the world collectables within one level	Bronze
Serious Collector	Collect all of the world collectables within a location	Bronze
World Set Complete!	Collect all of the world collectables within a world	Silver
Compulsive Collector	Collect all of the world collectables in the game	Gold
Suit Up!	Purchase a costume	Bronze
Dressed for Success!	Purchase all of the costumes	Silver
Four Star Costume!	Fully upgrade a costume	Bronze
World of Hurt!	Fully upgrade all of a world's costumes	Silver
Ultimate Cosmic Power!	Fully upgrade all of the costumes in the game	Gold
Challenge Addict	Play 50 challenges	Bronze
For The Win!	Win 50 challenges	Silver
The bigger they are . . .	Defeat the Brute	Bronze
Dizzy!	Defeat Roto	Bronze
Time for a Diet!	Defeat the Spawner	Bronze
Bad Dog!	Defeat the Bulldog	Bronze
Gold Hoarder	Amass 1,000 coins in the bank	Bronze
Richer than a McDuck!	Amass 10,000 coins in the bank	Silver
Along for the ride	Complete a level in multiplayer	Bronze
All Together Now!	Complete a level with four players	Bronze
Playing to win!	Defeat five players in a single level	Bronze
To infinity . . . and beyond!	Defeat another player by throwing them	Bronze
Keep 'em coming!	Defeat 100 enemies	Bronze
Anti-Virus!	Defeat 500 enemies	Silver
Giddy Up!	Defeat an enemy whilst riding an animal	Bronze
Freeze!	Defeat five enemies using a single Snowman power-up	Bronze
Boxing Clever	Defeat five enemies using a single Power Punch power-up	Bronze
Bad Hair Day	Defeat five enemies using a single Medusa power-up	Bronze
Rapid Fire	Defeat five enemies using a single Shooter power-up	Bronze
Tag! You're it!	Transfer a curse to another player	Bronze
Unstoppable!	Complete a level without respawning	Bronze
Old School	Complete a level without using help arrows	Bronze
Platinum Universe!	Collect all of the Trophies	Platinum

PRIMA Official Game Guide

Written by Michael Knight

Prima Games
An Imprint of Random House, Inc.
3000 Lava Ridge Court, St. 100
Roseville, CA 95661
www.primagames.com

Product Manager: Fernando Bueno

Design & Layout: Jamie Bryson

Maps: David Bueno

Copyeditor: Sara Wilson

Manufacturing: Stephanie Sanchez

Prima Games and the authors would like to thank Tina Kwan, Spencer Low, Amy M. Kreutzen, Hayley Green, Keely Brenner, Melanie Beard, Amber Anderson, Corina Sanchez, and Cyndi McGarrah for their tireless efforts in making this the best product it can be.

Important:

Michael Knight

Michael Knight has worked in the computer/video game industry since 1994 and has been an author with Prima Games for ten years, writing over 60 guides during this time. Michael has used both his degree in Military History and experience as a high school teacher to formulate and devise effective strategies and tactics for hit titles such as the Tom Clancy's Rainbow Six. Michael has also written Prima Official Game Guides for the many of the Lego games series, as well as a Disneyland travel guide.

When he is not busy at work on an upcoming strategy guide, Michael likes to spend time with his wife and six children at their home in Northern California.

We want to hear from you! E-mail comments and feedback to mknight@primagames.com.

ISBN: 978-0-307-89369-7
Printed in the United States of America
11 12 13 14 LL 10 9 8 7 6 5 4 3 2 1